The American Robin

NUMBER THIRTY-NINE

THE CORRIE HERRING HOOKS SERIES

Robin singing in pear tree. *Photo by Maslowski Wildlife Productions.*

ROLAND H. WAUER

The American Robin

UNIVERSITY OF TEXAS PRESS

AUSTIN

Requests for permission to reproduce material from this work should be sent
to Permissions, University of Texas Press, Box 7819, Austin, TX 78713-7819.

⊗

The paper used in this publication meets the minimum requirements of
American National Standard for Information Sciences—Permanence of Paper
for Printed Library Materials, ANSI Z39.48-1984.

LIBRARY OF CONGRESS CATALOGING IN PUBLICATION DATA

Wauer, Roland H.
The American robin / by Roland H. Wauer.—
p.   cm. — (The Corrie Herring Hooks series ; no. 39)
Includes bibliographical references (p.   ).
ISBN 0-292-79123-2 (cloth : alk. paper)
1. American robin.   I. Title.   II. Series.
QL696.P288 W38   1999
598.8′42—ddc21   98-25416

Contents

Acknowledgments

Several friends and colleagues have provided special assistance to me during the course of this project. Each of the following is gratefully acknowledged: Michael Husak and Terry Maxwell (Angelo State University) and Brent Ortego (Texas Parks and Wildlife Department) for help with obtaining references; Greg Lasley for up-to-date Texas records of *Turdus* thrushes; Andy O'Neil and Paul Palmer for information on recent breeding records in Texas; and John Sauer and Jane Fallon of the Patuxent Wildlife Research Center in Laurel, Maryland, for the maps. Several photographers kindly provided photographs used in this book, including Dave and Steve Maslowski, Jeffrey Rich, John and Gloria Tveten, and Tom J. Ulrich. The staff of the University of Texas Press has been extremely helpful throughout the publishing process. And last but not least, I thank my wife, Betty, for her constant support and interest.

The American Robin

Introduction

*Each time I study a new species I am amazed to find how much
I see after I have become thoroughly acquainted with it.*

NIKO TINBERGEN,
animal behaviorist and author of *Curious Naturalist*

*Robin is one of the most native and democratic of our birds; he
is one of the family, and seems much nearer to us than those
rare, exotic visitants . . . with their distant, high-bred ways.
Hardy, noisy, frolicsome, neighborly and domestic in his habits,
strong of wings, and bold in spirit, he is the pioneer of the
thrush family, and well worthy of the finer artists whose coming he heralds and in a measure prepares us for.*

JOHN BURROUGHS,
from *Wake-Robin*, 1913
("Wake-Robin" refers to the white trillium that blooms
in the eastern woods where Burroughs lived.)

Who in all of North America has not experienced our American
Robin up close and personal? Who has not watched Robin Redbreast in pursuit of earthworms on a lawn or open field? And
who has not enjoyed the robin's cheerful caroling?

No other songbird is so well-known as our American Robin.
It is as American as apple pie, baseball, and the Stars and
Stripes. The states of Connecticut, Michigan, and Wisconsin
have declared it their state bird, and in Canada, a pair of American Robins, or "le merle d'amerique" in French, grace two-
dollar bills.

Herbert Brandt, ornithologist and author of books about

birds from Alaska to Texas, writes in *Arizona and Its Bird Life,* "In my book of experience the bird that has displayed to me the most understandable avian behavior and appealing personality is the friendly, reliable Robin. Its daily fidelity, love of offspring, industry, flocking and migration behavior, familiarity, distribution, and many other attributes cause this bird, in my studies, to stand apart."

Although the Bald Eagle is America's national bird, and there are a handful of other species, such as the roadrunner, hummingbird, and chickadee, that may be more appealing, none is as widespread and as well-known as the American Robin. It resides on our lawns and in our gardens, fields, and pastures, as well as in the wild lands in which we recreate. It is known throughout North America, from the Arctic tundra to the humid Gulf lowlands, and from the Nor'east to the Baja Peninsula. It often is the only bird that as children we learn to call by name.

For me, after many years of enjoying nature, including untold experiences with wild birds, three robin incidents are especially meaningful.

I remember one early spring day along the Naval Oaks Trail in Florida's Gulf Islands National Seashore. The huge live oaks were filled with birdsongs, each species expressing their zeal for the coming season. Then ahead of me, somewhere to the left of the trail, I began to detect a strange, melodious hum. It took several minutes to reach a point on the trail where I was able to pinpoint the general location of the sound. By this time I began to see dozens of American Robins all about me, perched among the oaks, moving about from one spot to another, and arriving singly or in flocks from elsewhere.

I began to zero in on the principal source of the hum, soon recognizing that much of the harmony was supplied by mellow chips and partial songs of robins. I left the trail and slowly worked my way through the woods to where I could see a shallow pond just ahead. By now the sound was considerably louder, and I could also distinguish hundreds of minute splashings. A few feet closer and I was able to peer through the undergrowth

Robin drinking. *Photo by Jeffrey Rich.*

to across the pond. It wasn't until then that I understood the true cause of the hum. Hundreds of American Robins lined the shore or were perched on adjacent shrubs and trees. Those along the shore were bathing, dipping into the water and flipping it over their backs. They were spaced out shoulder to shoulder for 100 feet or more. Each bird seemed in pure delight! After a few dips and splashes, the bather would fly up to a low branch to shake and preen and chirp a few apparent notes of contentment. Its place on the shore was immediately taken by a waiting bird.

In watching the estimated thousand or more bathers that morning, I was struck by their good manners and patience in waiting their turn to bathe. Although I noticed some posturing during a bath, or an occasional bill jab or gaping when the next bather got too close, the entire flock of robins reminded me of lines of shoppers streaming to the checkout and waiting their turn. It was a marvelous experience!

On another spring day at Lassen Volcanic National Park in California, I was attracted to a pair of American Robins and five Steller's Jays, busily flying about an ancient ponderosa pine stump. I immediately assumed that the jays were engaged in nest robbery and the robins were attempting to defend their holdings. But when I got closer and had a better view, I discovered that instead, both species were busy capturing and eating flying carpenter ants as they emerged from three small holes in the huge stump. For several minutes I watched from about 80 feet away, while they continued their feeding activities. On most occasions the ants were taken immediately as they emerged, but at other times they were captured in flight. Both the jays and robins seemed perfectly capable of fly-catching.

There also were hundreds of nonwinged carpenter ants available, far more than the flying forms, but none of the birds took advantage of that food source. They picked only on the winged ants, assumedly males engaged in mating flights. The males die soon after mating to a larger queen ant that will then start a new colony or move into an already established colony. Apparently, the winged males possessed a different appeal from the more abundant nonwinged ants. Many became choice morsels for our American Robin.

Third was a childhood incident involving an American Robin that first ignited my interest in birds. It occurred in Idaho Falls, Idaho, my hometown, where I lived until moving to California when I was 14 years old. Receiving a bow and arrows for my twelfth birthday, I soon was practicing on almost any target available. Cans and cardboard bears and dragons were most popular, and I got to the point where I could shoot reasonably straight, at least within a dozen feet or so. Then came the day when I was shooting in a nearby field, where several American Robins were hunting earthworms, and I decided to use one of the red-breasted birds as a target.

In retrospect, I am sure that I gave little thought to such behavior and probably didn't believe that I would really be able to hit so small a target, but I drew back my bow and let an arrow fly. My target, more than 200 feet away, was cleanly pierced by my arrow. As you might surmise, that youngster ran up to his dead prey with wonder that he had struck down so small a target at such a distance. But on picking up the dead and bleeding robin to retrieve my arrow, I remember how distraught I suddenly became. I was holding a limp ball of feathers that only seconds before had been a wonderful, living creature, representing a bird that I had seen and listened to many times before. With one thoughtless action I had destroyed that vision. I remember how sad I was afterward. I put up my bow and arrows that day, and since then have watched our feathered friends only with admiration and respect.

Years later, through a questionnaire to members of the American Birding Association, I discovered that 27 percent of all birders began their hobby because of a "spark bird," an encounter with a single bird that ignited their interest (Wauer 1991). The

American Robin was my spark bird that led me to an exciting world of natural history.

Claim to Fame

The American Robin literally sets the standard for all other songbirds. Nature lovers all across North America commonly judge the sizes of all other birds by whether they are the same size, larger, or smaller than the American Robin. The robin's breast provides us with the characteristic robin-red color. Even their eggs are robin's-egg blue. The term "robin snow" is used for a light spring snow coming after the return of the American Robin.

Even in the music world, several songs highlight the American Robin. The earliest one—"When the Robins Nest Again"— was written by Frank Howard in 1883. More recent examples include "Robin and Roses," a 1936 ditty sung by Bing Crosby; the more upbeat "Rockin' Robin"; and Harry Woods's 1926 classic, "When the Red, Red Robin Comes Bob, Bob, Bobbin' Along." Woods's robin song, a wonderful tune that almost everyone knows from childhood, may even provide us with a sort of standard for happiness songs.

There also are numerous robin nursery rhymes. Although many of these may refer to the European Robin, they nevertheless were memorized and quoted by an untold number of American youngsters. Most are anonymous. Three of them I remember from my childhood:

> The north wind doth blow,
> And we shall have snow,
> And what will poor robin do then,
> Poor thing?
> He'll sit in a barn,
> To keep himself warm,
> And hide his head under his wing,
> Poor thing!
>
> from "The North Wind Doth Blow"

and

> Who killed Cock Robin?
> "I," said the sparrow,
> "With my bow and arrow,
> I killed Cock Robin."
>
> Who saw him die?
> "I," said the fly,
> "With my little eye,
> I saw him die."
>
> from "Who Killed Cock Robin?"

and

> Little Robin Redbreast
> Came to visit me;
> This is what he whistled,
> Thank you for my tea.

Robin Facts and Fiction

As with many of our wild creatures, some robin facts are stranger than fiction.

Facts

AVERAGE ESTIMATED LIFE SPAN: 1 year and 2 months

MAXIMUM KNOWN AGE: 17 years

LENGTH: 9 to 11 inches

WINGSPAN: 14.75 to 16.5 inches

WEIGHT: 2.5 to 3 ounces

ADULT AVERAGE BODY TEMPERATURE: 109.7 degrees F

FLIGHT SPEED: 17 to 32 miles per hour

NUMBER OF FEATHERS: about 2,900

SONG DESCRIPTION: "cheer-up, cheerily, cheer-up, cheer-up, cheerily"

SONG IN CYCLES PER SECOND: 2,200 to 3,300

NESTING CYCLE: 27 to 38 days, including 3 to 10 days for nest building, 13 to 15 days for incubation, and 13 to 15 days of nest life

NEST SIZE: 6 to 7 inches across the top and 3 inches high, with an inner cup about 4 inches wide and 2.5 inches deep

CLUTCH SIZE: normally 4, but ranging from 3 to 7

FOOD FOR AVERAGE BROOD: 3.2 pounds in total or 356 feedings daily

The robin name was derived from the little red-breasted European Robin, closely related to wheatears but totally unrelated to our American Robin. Early settlers to North America bestowed that cherished name on the red-breasted American thrush because of its friendly manner and close relationship with people, behavior that reminded them of the European Robin back home.

The earlier term, "Robin," is a common British nickname for a close family member, but it was initially derived from the French "Robert," probably introduced to Great Britain by the invading Normans in the eleventh century. Prior to then, the British robin was called "ruddock," the name used by Shakespeare. Early French Canadians referred to the American Robin as "merle," a name also used for the European Blackbird. Two German names for the American Robin were also used: "die Wanderdrossell," translated as "the wanderer," and "Rotkehlchen," or "redbreast." Some other early Americans called it "wandering thrush."

To scientists, the American Robin is *Turdus migratorius*. "*Turdus*" is Latin for thrush, and "*migratorius*" is Latin for migratory, a name "derived from *migro*, to move from one place to another," according to Edward Gruson in *Words for Birds: A Lexicon of North American Birds with Biogeographical Notes*.

Fiction

There are innumerable stories about the robin, ranging from how it was named to its out-of-the-ordinary behavior. For instance, Laura Martin, in *The Folklore of Birds*, writes: "Legend tells us that the robin received its red breast when it plucked a thorn from Christ's crown on his way to Calvary and the flowing blood turned his breast red." She also explains that "many cultures" believed that the robin's nest is sacred, that if you bother it on its nest, "you would get sick and give bloody milk."

Other versions of deriving bad luck from injuring robins were included in *A Dictionary of Superstitions*, by Iona Opie and Moira Tatem.

"A popular belief in many Country places, that it is unlucky to kill or keep Robins."

"Very few children in this town would hurt a redbreast, as it is considered unlucky to do so; this bird being entitled to kindness—above every other."

"Whoever kills a robin redbreast will never have good luck were they to live a thousand years."

"It used to be said to children that if they ever took robin's eggs—their little fingers would be sure to grow crooked."

"If you break a robin's leg, your leg will be broken; and if you break a robin's wing, your arm will be broken."

In the 1612 play *The White Devil*, by John Webster, we find the following verse:

> Call for the robin redbreast and the wren.
> Since o'er shady groves they hover,
> And with leaves and flowers do cover
> The friendless bodies of unburied men.

Even Shakespeare evoked the ancient belief that a robin would cover unburied bodies when he wrote in *Cymbeline:*

> Out-sweeten'd not thy breath: the ruddock would
> With charitable bill,—O bill, sore shaming
> Those rich-left heirs that let their fathers lie
> Without a monument!—bring thee all this;
> Yea, and furr'd moss besides, when flowers are none,
> To winter-ground thy corse.

Female partial albino robin. *Photo by Tom J. Ulrich.*

Description

Appearance

THE American Robin is the largest of our North American thrushes, 9 to 11 inches in length and with a wingspan between 14.75 and 16.5 inches. Robin weights range from 64.8 to 84.2 grams, about 2.5 to 3 ounces. For comparison, other North American bird weights range from a low of 2.4 to 4.5 g for the Ruby-throated Hummingbird to 4,536 to 13,608 g for the Brown Pelican. Examples of mean weights include 10 g for the House Wren, 64.2 g for the Evening Grosbeak, 113.5 g for the American Kestrel, 1,870 g for the Great Blue Heron, and 3,000 g for the Golden Eagle. Approximately 15 percent of a bird's weight is flight muscle, and only 4 percent is the bird's hollow bones.

Adult American Robins possess the characteristic plumage of a clear brick- to rufous-red breast, blackish head with incomplete white eye rings, white chin with black streaks, yellow bill with a barely noticeable black tip, olive to brownish gray or black back and wings, white lower belly, and blackish tail. The tail corners are white in eastern birds but plain in western birds. American Robin plumage also varies slightly with sex and geographic range. Males normally are darker with more intense colors than the females. Northeastern birds are darkest, and southern robins are somewhat lighter.

The American Robin's breast is unquestionably its most distinguishing feature. Like almost all the other thrushes, juveniles possess a characteristic spotted breast: large black spots on a pale orange to reddish background. Fall birds, adults and young alike, often look strange because of their freshly molted breast feathers, which may show whitish edges that appear scalloped. Robins go through one complete molt each year between late

July and early October. By the following spring, however, the whitish edges are worn off, and the breast is bright red.

Albinism in the American Robin is rare, but an ardent robin observer sooner or later will find one with albinistic features. Occasionally, totally white birds with pink eyes, indicating a total lack of pigments, are found. More often, partially albino birds, with all-white plumage but normal eyes, or heavily spotted birds are seen. The white markings may come and go, however. Bird banders report recapturing normal birds that had been partially albino in a previous molt.

Ira Gabrielson and Stanley Jewett, in *Birds of Oregon,* report "well-established annual outbreaks of newspaper reports of albino robins" in the Portland area. They write: "There seems to be a marked albinistic strain in the birds of that locality, as we see one or more albinos each season and collected several."

Melanistic birds, those with an excess of black pigment in their plumage, are truly exceptional. Melanism, the opposite of albinism, is reported for only 29 species of North American birds, very few compared to the more than 400 species with reported albinism. Rarely, partial albinistic and melanistic characteristics may occur on the same individual.

Feathers are a bird's most distinguishing feature, a characteristic that no other creatures possess. Robins possess a total of approximately 2,900 feathers, in the midrange compared with only about 1,000 for the Ruby-throated Hummingbird, 2,000 to 2,500 for woodpeckers and doves, 6,500 for gulls, 12,000 for ducks, and 25,000 for swans.

Flight

Bird flight is one of nature's most outstanding miracles. Birds provided the perfect model for the airplane industry—wings for support and steering, tail for control, and an internal mechanism for power. But robin flight is unique, possessing a design and appearance all its own.

It is relatively easy to identify a flying robin at a considerable distance by its distinct straight-ahead, full-breasted flight pattern. It does not rush forward like a starling or House Sparrow, mix rapid with slow wing strokes like shrikes, undulate its flight like woodpeckers and goldfinches, zigzag like feeding swallows, flap and soar like numerous raptors, or maneuver like hummingbirds.

Winsor Marrett Tyler, author of "Eastern Robin," in Arthur Cleveland Bent's *Life Histories of North American Thrushes, Kinglets, and Their Allies,* provides us with a wonderful description of the robin's flight:

> He flies with very straight back, like a runner with head thrown back, and his breast appears puffed out, expanded, giving a curved outline to the underparts in contrast to the long, straight line of the back and tail. The wings, at the end of the stroke, are not clapped close to the sides, as in the flight of a blackbird or woodpecker. The robin nevertheless accomplishes a full stroke by flapping the tips of the wings well backward so that, at the end of the stroke, the primary feathers of each side are nearly parallel, while the wrist remains out a little way from the body. The wings move rapidly and regularly and there is commonly no soaring or sailing.

A robin's normal flight speed ranges from 17 to 32 mph. Examples of a few other birds' flight speeds vary from 15 to 20 mph for the Chipping Sparrow, about 27 mph for the Ruby-throated Hummingbird, about 44 mph for the Northern Flicker, 38 to 49 mph for the European Starling, 28 to 55 mph for the Killdeer, 44 to 59 mph for ducks, 22 to 60 mph for the Barn Swallow, about 90 mph for the Common Loon, and 39 to 180 mph for the Peregrine Falcon.

Voice

American Robins sing loudest and sweetest at dawn and dusk, especially in spring and early summer when nesting. Throughout their range, the robin's song is usually the first birdsong heard in the mornings and the last song heard in the evenings. Aldo Leopold used a sensitive photometer to determine the light intensity during the first morning songs of 20 songbirds near Madison, Wisconsin (Leopold and Eynon 1961). He discovered that the American Robin begins its morning songs with as little as 0.023 foot-candle of light at 3:15 a.m. on clear April mornings. He also confirmed that cloudy conditions delayed morning songs and that bright moonlight at night enticed birds to sing. American Robins also sing throughout the summer months and into September or October, when most other birds are silent.

Although the male robin is credited with the majority of robin serenades, both sexes do sing, and they sing most frequently just before the hatching of each brood. Donald Stokes, in *A Guide to the Behavior of Common Birds,* points out, however, that many songs of male robins do "not seem to be associated with any particular aspect of the bird's life. In most birds, song is used to advertise territory, to attract a mate, or both."

The interpretation or phonics of robin songs varies with the listener. To my ear, the typical American Robin sings, "Cheer-up, cheerily, cheer-up, cheer-up, cheerily." Other writers have interpreted robin songs somewhat differently. Tyler states, "Cheerily, cheery is a favorite rendering of his song, aptly suggesting by sound and meaning the joyous tenor of the phrases, and the liquid quality of the notes." John Terres, in *The Audubon Society Encyclopedia of North American Birds,* translates its song as "cheer-up, cheer, cheer, cheer-up." Stokes describes its song as "cheeriup, cheerily, cheeriup." Dr. Leroy Titus Weeks (in Bent's *Life Histories*) provides us with a very different interpretation:

> Pilly wink, polly wog, poodle, poodle,
> Pollywog, poodle, pillywink, pillywink,
> Poodle, poodle, pillywink, pollywog,
> Poodle, poodle.

Whatever one's interpretation is of the robin's full-voiced song, everyone can agree that it is joyful and cheerful, an outpouring of liquid notes that is full of enthusiasm.

Several naturalists have also described a rain song, a soft, quiet rendition of its more typical song. The rain song precedes a summer storm and may also be in response to decreased intensity of light. Stokes also transcribes this song, sung with approaching clouds, as "more wet, cheer up."

In a more detailed description of robin songs, ornithologist Aretas A. Saunders, a specialist in birdsongs, describes song phrasing (in Bent) thusly:

> Individual robins differ from each other in the phrases they use
> and the order in which they sing them. While many of the phrases
> are common to robins in general, nearly every individual will have
> some peculiar phrase. The average number of phrases used by
> one individual is about 10, but there is great variation: one bird I
> listened to for some time had apparently only 2; another had but
> 3; while a third unusual bird had 26. Two- and three-note phrases
> are a rule, but a single note used as a phrase is not uncommon.
> Only twice have I heard a phrase of four notes.

Collins and Boyajians, in *Familiar Garden Birds of America,* write that the well-sustained robin song "averages two phrases per second, with an almost imperceptible pause every few phrases."

The human ear is most efficient in detecting notes between 1,000 and 4,000 cycles per second (cps). The highest note on a piano has a frequency of about 4,000 cps. The American Robin sings between 2,200 and 3,300 cps, a little lower than the Red-eyed Vireo (2,375 to 5,125 cps) or the various warblers that average about 5,350 cps. The ranges of songbird frequencies vary considerably:

NORTHERN CARDINAL: 1,500 to 4,500 cps

EASTERN WOOD-PEWEE: 4,125 to 4,375 cps

LEAST FLYCATCHER: 3,500 to 5,125 cps

SONG SPARROW: 1,800 to 9,000 cps

OVENBIRD: 2,500 to 9,000 cps

BLACKPOLL WARBLER: 8,050 to 10,225 cps

EUROPEAN STARLING: 650 to 15,000 cps

HOUSE SPARROW: 675 to 18,000 cps

American Robins also possess a variety of call notes. Stokes discusses four common ones that may be used by either sex: The "teck-call" is a short and shrill "teeeek teeeek," often repeated many times and usually given in situations of possible danger. The "tuk-tuk-tuk-call" is a series of short, guttural notes, also given to signal danger or disturbance. The "teacher-call" is a rapidly repeated series of harsh notes, like "teach each each" or "teach each each each each—ooch oochooch," given with increasing volume, and used in a variety of situations. The "eee-call" is a high, thin whistle that resembles that of Cedar Waxwings. It often is used by robins "in flight to their evening communal roosts in fall and winter."

It is obvious that American Robins call often: when they take flight or land, to inform others of their movement and give their locations, and to inform others of food or predators. Also, a louder call or increased rate of calling will usually attract other robins to see what the excitement is all about.

Robins also are one of the few songbirds that will continue singing at their roost, at least during the early mornings and evenings, until fall. Once the young of the year are present, this provides them with a learning experience. The practice of sub-songs by the youngsters can begin at about 21 days of age; it subsides in winter but is perfected the following spring.

Anyone who has paid even the slightest attention to birds has heard and, undoubtedly, enjoyed the American Robin's flutelike songs and pert calls, and forevermore may the reader associate its cheerful caroling with happiness.

Physiology

The internal organs of the American Robin, and of most other birds, have evolved primarily in response to flight. Every aspect of the robin's biology is profoundly affected by the ability to move through the air. The principal requirements include lightness, streamlining, strength, and highly effective systems of circulation, respiration, digestion, and excretion.

The avian skeleton, which houses the internal organs and provides anchorage for muscles, is an amazing structure. It is built of relatively large, rigid, hollow bones that are lightweight and strong. Rigidity of the backbone allows for effective flight and an easy bipedal posture. The hollow bones, like a hollow girder, are extremely light but strong. The hollow bones also provide interconnected passageways from the relatively small lungs to all parts of the body. Besides the lungs and the pneumatic (hollow) sternum, pectoral girdle bones, and humerus, birds also possess one unpaired and four pairs of air sacs. Head to tail they include the paired cervical, unpaired interclavical, and paired anterior thoracic, posterior thoracic, and abdominal air sacs. A bird can actually breathe through a broken humerus. The avian respiratory system is more highly developed than that of any other group of animals. A robin's lungs are only 2 percent of its body volume, compared with 5 percent in man, and their air sacs are 10 percent of its body volume, or about 80 percent of the total volume of its respiratory system.

Robins normally breathe at a rate of 45 times per minute, but this can increase five- or six-fold with additional activity and higher body temperature. William A. Dunson discovered that American Robins living at 9,500 feet elevation had lungs averaging 41 percent larger than those living at sea level, and R. A. Norris and F. S. Williamson found that heart weights of birds at high elevations in the Sierra Nevada averaged one-fourth heavier than in those same species living at low elevations.

Since birds do not sweat, they must eliminate excess body heat by panting, speeding up the ventilation of respiratory passageways. During flight, the additional heat stress is handled largely by the air sacs. The heart, in direct response to the high respiratory requirements imposed by flight, beats faster. A robin's resting heart beat of 570 times per minute may exceed 1,000 beats per minute during stressful conditions.

The robin's normal body temperature is 109.7 degrees F, although that may fluctuate 6 degrees over a 24-hour period. Comparisons for normal body temperatures include 110 F for the House Sparrow, 107.4 F for the Common Raven, 106.7 F for the European Starling, 102 F for the Ruby-throated Hummingbird, and 99.9 F for the Brown Pelican.

Robins often are found in very cold locations, because they stay put at choice feeding areas year-round or arrive early in spring, or in very warm summering locations. Both require a constant body temperature. Since all birds are endothermic (warm-blooded), hot environmental conditions may be more stressful than cold ones. Therefore, to avoid overheating and death, they often seek shade and become inactive during the middle of the day.

Avian metabolism also has evolved rapid digestion and efficient elimination of waste products. Bird kidneys are generally twice the size of kidneys in comparable mammals. Paul Ehrlich and colleagues, in *The Birder's Handbook,* point out that the "main function of a bird's kidneys is to remove from the blood the nitrogen-containing wastes formed during the breakdown of proteins—and to do so while maintaining the proper balance of water, salts, and other materials in the body. In arid environments birds can remove these wastes while passing very little water in the urine." Both digestive and excretory systems are voided from a common chamber, the cloaca. There is no urinary bladder in birds; instead, the walls of the cloaca reabsorb much of the water and return it to the blood, another method of economizing in birds.

Even a bird's reproductive organs are lightweight and efficient. The male's reproductive structures are dominated by paired testes, while those of the female include paired ovaries, although normally only the left one develops. As birds come into their breeding cycle, these structures will rapidly increase in size to as much as 50 times that of nonbreeders. Copulation is accomplished by direct cloacal contact when the male momentarily mounts the back of the female. Eggs are produced by the ovary and passed into the oviduct, where they are fertilized.

When ready for deposition, they usually are laid a day apart until the clutch is complete.

Senses

Avian senses vary greatly in comparison with those of humans; sight and hearing are more highly developed, touch is about the same, and taste and smell are less developed.

Eyesight in birds is far more proficient than in humans. Joel Carl Welty, in *The Life of Birds,* claims that a bird "can gain more information about [its] surroundings through its eyes than through its other sense organs together." It can detect the direction, distance, size, shape, brightness, color hue, color intensity, three-dimensional perception, and motion of an object. Robin eyes are placed so that they see in a much wider angle than humans, allowing them to detect predators better. However, most bird eyes are only slightly movable; a robin must cock its head to search for worms (see the section Feeding for details).

Hearing in most birds tends to be more sensitive to faint vibrations and differences in intensity and to a higher range of frequencies than in humans. The human ear can detect sounds ranging from about 16 to 20,000 cycles per second, but a bird's hearing range extends from about 40 to 29,000 cycles per second. Birds seem also to possess a better sense of time discrimination; Welty points out that birds are "able to hear and respond to rapid fluctuations in song about ten times as rapidly as man can." But a primary role of the avian ear, insofar as flight is concerned, is maintaining equilibrium.

A bird's sense of touch includes refinements and adaptations to its way of life. Welty states that it "is likely that a bird's skin possesses sense endings, much like those in man, which pick up touch, pain, heat, and cold. Such endings are usually more abundant in skin that lacks feathers."

Taste and smell are poorly developed in birds. Taste includes salt, sour, bitter, and sweet. Smell, at least for passerines, is limited to the bird's ability to test food held in its mouth.

Distribution

AMERICAN Robins are one of the most widespread songbirds in the Western Hemisphere. They are one of our most adaptable species, occurring from the Arctic to the tropics. Breeding birds can be found from sea level to mountain treelines, in Alaska through Canada to Newfoundland, south to California, Texas, and South Carolina, and in the highlands of Mexico and Guatemala. Temperature is a key factor in their existence, for robins need thawed ground so that they can dig earthworms. Wintering birds may occur from British Columbia to Newfoundland and southward throughout the United States, Mexico, and Central America.

Summer

Robins have not always been so widely distributed in North America. There has been a well-documented shift in their breeding range since about the turn of the century. Frank L. Farley reports robin increases to the north:

> During the last half century the robin has increased in Alberta [Canada] at least 100 percent. This is in about the same ratio as the country has been settled. When the hard prairie lands were broken up, it was noted that earthworms were absent, but with the arrival of the settlers, it was not long before the worms began to appear, especially in the gardens surrounding the buildings. The birds increased in numbers at about the same rate as the growth of garden space. It is believed that the settlers inadvertently introduced the worms with the potted plants and shrubs which they brought with them.

Tyler (in Bent) describes the robin's remarkable range extension in South Carolina:

> Early in the present century the robin, in the South Carolina Piedmont, was regarded as a harbinger of cold weather. They descended from the mountains and the more northern areas to feed on chinaberries especially. . . . As the smaller towns installed civic waterworks and water was available for lawns, and incidentally for earthworms, robins apparently began to spread, as inhabitants of cities and towns, until they may now be found in summer, even far down on the coast plain.

American Robin populations in Texas experienced a similar change, according to Harry C. Oberholser in *The Bird Life of Texas:*

> During the historic period, the Robin has been only a local breeder in Texas, except in the forested eastern quarter. Most of the state is too hot, dry, and deficient in woodlands to induce enthusiastic nesting. Between 1925 and 1940 there was an increase in tree planting and lawn sprinkling in Texas communities. As a result of these well-spaced trees, increased humidity, and mud for nest-wall construction, breeders increased in north Texas and spread south to Waco, Austin, San Antonio, and by 1967 had reached Corpus Christi.

Even more recently, robin nests were found in Falfurrias, Texas, in the eighties and in Kingsville, Texas, in 1993, locations southwest of Corpus Christi, according to Paul Palmer (personal communication). In Mississippi, Toups and Jackson reported the first confirmed nesting records for that state, from Lizana in 1983 and Saucier, in north Harrison County, in 1986.

That same scenario occurred all across North America. The robin, once found only at open areas within the forests and woodlands, became a welcome neighbor wherever settlement occurred. Glover M. Allen, in *Birds and Their Attributes,* claimed that the planting of apple orchards in Oklahoma was chiefly responsible for bringing robins into that state. Tracy Storer points out that there were no breeding bird records for Marin County,

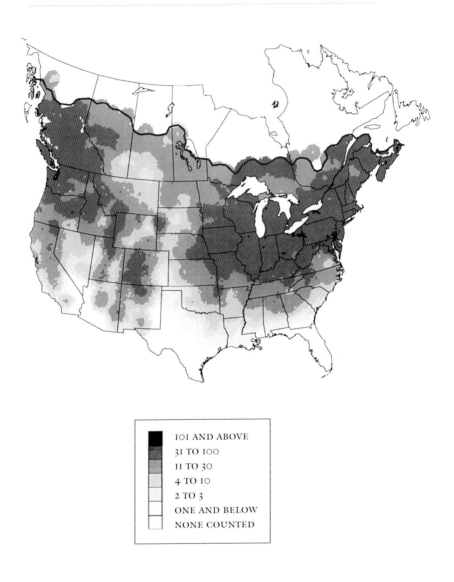

■	101 AND ABOVE
▓	31 TO 100
▒	11 TO 30
░	4 TO 10
	2 TO 3
	ONE AND BELOW
	NONE COUNTED

MAP A. Breeding distribution, 1997.
Courtesy of Patuxent Wildlife Research Center,
Department of the Interior

Winter scene. *Photo by Jeffrey Rich/Global.*

California, until 1915. Before then, robins nested only in "those parts of the State where damp meadows, with short grass in which the adults might seek their forage, persisted during the summer months."

It is clear that the American Robin is one of the few native species to have benefited from human development. Each new farm that broke up the hard prairie sod, each village and town with their suburban neighborhoods, parks, gardens, and orchards, provided them with new opportunities. By the thirties, our American Robin had become North America's most widespread songbird.

Although the species experienced a setback during the fifties, with the indiscriminate use of DDT (discussed later in Enemies and Threats), it is likely that it is more abundant today than at any time in the past. Breeding bird surveys provide us with the best and most up-to-date data on their summertime distribution. Map A, obtained through the courtesy of the National Biological Survey, provides an updated version of the map that was utilized by Chandler Robbins, Danny Bystrak, and Paul Geissler in *The Breeding Bird Survey: Its First Fifteen Years, 1965–1979*. This map illustrates the American Robin's continentwide distribution as well as the mean relative abundance of breeding birds from 1965 to 1996. The authors report that during their 15-year timeframe, American Robin populations experienced "strong and significant recovery across the continent in both the Eastern and Central regions, especially in the Northern Plains, the Great Lakes, and the Southeastern States." These same data are used by Frank Graham, Jr., in a 1994 *American Birds* article, "What Is the State of the State Birds?" Graham reports that in Connecticut, Wisconsin, and Michigan, American Robin populations increased by 16 percent, 31 percent, and 45 percent, respectively.

Winter

The American Robin is not the typical wintering songbird. While many birds that winter in the southern states are more apparent and less shy than they are on their breeding grounds, the opposite is true for the robin. In summer robins frequent lawns and gardens, but in winter they normally stay in large flocks that prefer wildlands, often leaving residential areas immediately when disturbed.

Wintering robins generally move to lower and warmer areas where there is a greater abundance of berries, but a few can be found in many of the same areas in which they spent their summers. According to the American Ornithologists' Union 1983 *Check-list of North American Birds*, the American Robin's wintering range extends from:

> southern Alaska (casually), southwestern British Columbia, the northern United States (at least irregularly in the northmost states) and Newfoundland south to southern Baja California (casually to Guadalupe Island), throughout Mexico (rarely to the Yucatan Peninsula and Isla Holbox) to Guatemala, and to southern Texas, the Gulf Coast, southern Florida, Bermuda and (at least irregularly) western Cuba, casually to the northern Bahama Islands (south to San Salvador).

The greatest numbers of wintering robins can be found in the southern United States, avoiding higher elevations where average minimum temperatures in January drop below 5 degrees F, as well as areas receiving less than 8 inches of annual precipitation.

Perhaps, the best indicators of winter bird numbers are the Christmas bird counts (CBCs) that are taken within 15-mile-diameter areas during two-week periods at Christmastime all across North America. Map B (courtesy of National Biological Survey) shows the winter distribution of American Robins from CBCs throughout North America in 1997. In summarizing robin numbers from CBCs, Terry Root states, "Wintering Robins are wanderers, often covering extensive areas in their search for food. And when their food supplies are low or exhausted in the north, it can result in massive invasions into new areas. All the Gulf Coastal states always host significant wintering populations, but experience major invasions only occasionally."

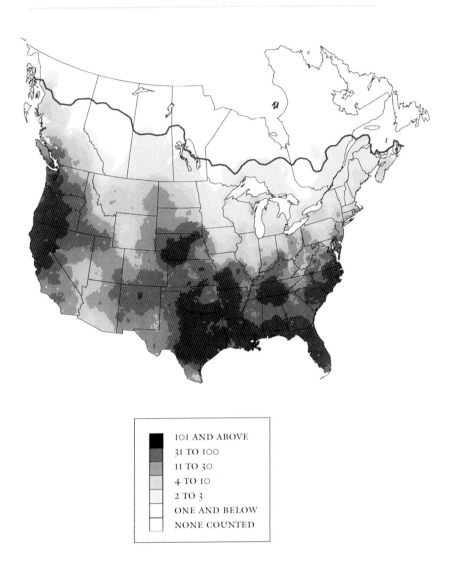

ONE AND BELOW

NONE COUNTED

MAP B. Winter distribution, 1997.
Courtesy of Patuxent Wildlife Research Center,
Department of the Interior

In *Louisiana Birds,* George Lowery, Jr., points out that robins arrive in numbers in mid-October and remain until early March: "In the first half of the winter robins are most numerous in the wooded swamps, but by the time January arrives they begin to enter the cities and towns to feed on lawns and golf courses."

Wintering robin numbers can be extensive. More than a million robins were reported on a 40-acre swampland tract in Alabama in the twenties. Welty recorded a winter roost of about one million birds in Virginia's Dismal Swamp. Bent reports that 50,000 robins spent the night "in low evergreen bushes, in a cypress swamp" in Florida. The 1980–1981 CBC for Burnet County, Texas, tallied 1,620,000 robins. Gordon Bolander recorded a "large winter roost in Lakeside Park, Oakland, California, in which he estimated that there were 165,000 birds" (Bent). But the largest known wintertime congregation was reported by P. C. Peterson (1965) in Missouri: "The most dramatic roost by far was the one located near Fertile, Missouri, about 60 miles southwest of St. Louis. It was visited several times and the number of birds present from late December to mid-January was conservatively estimated by sectional counts at 3,500,000."

Some altitudinal winter movement occurs, as well. I found that robins descended into Death Valley from the adjacent Panamint Mountains with each snowstorm in the highlands. At those times, flocks of 10 to 70 birds remained at Furnace Creek Ranch, situated below sea level, "for a few hours or many days," depending upon the storm.

Some winters, a larger than normal robin population remains in the northern states. Chandler Robbins, in summarizing the 1956 winter season, attributes the larger northern populations to "(1) unusually high productivity in the preceding season, productivity that increased population pressure everywhere in the eastern United States; (2) exceptionally good winter food reserves in the north; and (3) exceptionally early northbound migration, reflecting an unusually mild winter."

However, because of the robin's wandering nature, the species is not as faithful to its wintering grounds as most other songbirds. A 12-year study by William Wharton in South Carolina revealed that none of 72 banded robins returned a second year. Conversely, Wharton found that 12.3 percent of 81 banded Hermit Thrushes, 8.4 percent of 296 Song Sparrows, 2.3 percent of 347 Dark-eyed Juncos, and 19.7 percent of 3,753 Chipping Sparrows returned for at least a second winter.

Other North American Thrushes

THE subfamily of thrushes and their allies (Turdinae) is practically cosmopolitan, absent only from New Zealand, a few Polynesian islands, Antarctica, and the frigid parts of the Arctic. It includes some of the most highly regarded songbirds in the world. Oliver Austin, Jr., in *Song Birds of the World*, writes, "No other family has so many members famed for their music—the Nightingale, Song Thrush, Hermit Thrush, and Wood Thrush, to name a few." He also provides us with a thumbnail sketch of the thrushes:

> The thrushes are slightly larger, chunkier birds than the Old World warblers and the flycatchers, and typically have the tarsus unscaled or "booted." Though essentially insectivorous, thrushes do not catch insects in flight. [The apparent exception is my observation of robins feeding on flying carpenter ants at Lassen.] They feed on the ground as well as in trees, and eat more vegetable food, particularly fruit, than warblers and flycatchers do. All build open cup nests, usually in trees or bushes, some on the ground, and a few in rock crevices and tree cavities.

Nine genera of thrushes occur regularly in North America: *Luscinia*, Siberian Rubythroat and Bluethroat; *Oenanthe*, Northern Wheatear; *Sialia*, bluebirds; *Myadestes*, solitaires; *Catharus*, Nightingale-Thrushes, Veery, and several thrushes; *Hylocichla*, Wood Thrush; *Turdus*, several additional thrushes and robins; *Ixoreus*, Varied Thrush; and *Ridgwayia*, Aztec Thrush.

A total of 15 *Turdus* thrushes and robins occur naturally in North America, including the West Indies (see Table 1). Only four species of *Turdus* thrushes have been found within the United States: Clay-colored, White-throated, Rufous-backed, and American robins. Clay-colored Robins are rare but regular

visitors to South Texas, actually nesting successfully at Bentsen–
Rio Grande Valley State Park. The first U.S. record of a White-
throated Robin was at Laguna Vista, Texas, in February 1991
(Lasley and Krzywonski, 1991); in Spring 1998 at least four were
recorded at Bentsen–Rio Grande Valley State Park and Santa
Ana National Wildlife Refuge. Rufous-backed Robins are also
accidental, having been recorded only a few times in Arizona
and Texas. The American Robin is the only common *Turdus*
thrush in the United States and Canada. It, essentially, is our
only representative of this tropical genus and therefore, in spite
of its abundance, is of truly outstanding status.

TABLE I

North American Thrushes and Robins of the Genus *Turdus*

SPECIES	COMMON NAME
T. nigrescens	Sooty Robin
T. infuscatus	Black Robin
T. plebejus	Mountain Robin
T. fumigatus	Cocoa Thrush
T. obsoletus	Pale-vented Thrush
T. grayi	Clay-colored Robin
T. nadigenis	Bare-eyed Robin
T. jamaicensis	White-eyed thrush
T. assimilis	White-throated Robin
T. rufopalliatus	Rufous-backed Robin
T. rufitorques	Rufous-collared Robin
T. migratorius	American Robin
T. swalesi	La Selle Thrush
T. aurantius	White-chinned Thrush
T. plumbeus	Red-legged Thrush

Names and order as listed by American Ornithologists' Union, 1983, *Check-list of North
American Birds.*

American Robin Behavior

Behavior can be defined as the sum of the ways in which an organism reacts to its environment. Almost any question that one might have about a bird's activities involves the study of its behavior. How does a robin maintain a viable population? How does it find its food? How does it maintain its feathers? How does it communicate? How does it survive in a world of seasonal changes, competitors, and predators?

Yet the American Robin is a bird of behavioral contradictions. It possesses an amazing tolerance of human beings, even building its nests on and adjacent to our homes, yet it is exceedingly wild in its natural forest environment. In spring and summer robins feed primarily on the ground, searching for earthworms and insects, but in fall and winter they feed principally on berries and other fruits on trees, shrubs, and vines. In addition, unlike any of the other passerines, male robins roost together year-round, even in spring when defending their nesting territory during all the daylight hours.

Feeding

A red-breasted bird running about a lawn or field, stopping to stand upright and alert, watching for any movement after each spurt, then running off in a different direction, is displaying classic American Robin hunting behavior. It may actually take a zigzag route in its search. Every now and then it will cock its head sideways to see an insect, spider, or earthworm better; it may suddenly run forward to grab its prey.

Head-cocking enhances its view of the ground. Since robin eyes are only slightly movable, it must tilt its head to focus on objects. Head-tilting allows images to be focused on the retina, offering the greatest visual acuity. What appears to be listening is actually careful looking. Occasionally one can witness a tug-of-war as the robin applies only so much pressure to pull an earthworm gradually from its burrow.

There has long been an argument about whether the American Robin is using sight or sound in its search for earthworms. The verdict is conclusive that sight, not sound, is employed. Frank Heppner performed a variety of tests before he concluded that vibrations, odors, and sounds were of no value to birds seeking earthworms. He recorded and played back very low-intensity sounds made by burrowing earthworms with no effect. He discovered that robins "nonchalantly ate foods smelling like rotten eggs, decaying meats, rancid butter, and the absolutely worst smell of all bad smells, mercaptoacetic acid, which has been described as a cross between sewer gas, rotten cabbage, a skunk, and a stinkbug." He also discovered that robins did not peck at artificially produced earthworm holes. But when pieces of dead earthworms were placed just inside artificial burrows, they readily found and removed the pieces.

The year-round diet of American Robins includes animals 42 percent of the time and plants 58 percent of the time, according to Alexander Martin, Herbert Zim, and Arnold Nelson's *American Wildlife and Plants: A Guide to Wildlife Food Habits.* They found that the robin's principal "items of animal food are caterpillars, beetles (particularly ground beetles, weevils, and dung beetles), and earthworms. The balance of the animal diet was made up largely of true bugs, flies, sowbugs, snails, spiders, termites, millipedes, and centipedes." The chief plant foods varied across the country. In the Northeast, cultivated and wild cherries, dogwood, sumac, and blackgum were most popular; chinaberry and blackberry were most popular in the Southeast; holly, palmetto, blackgum, chinaberry, and beautyberry in Florida; hackberry, cultivated and wild grapes, and cultivated and wild cherries in the eastern prairies; cedar, hackberry, and Russian olive in the Intermountain West; and peppertree, cultivated grapes, prune, and cultivated and wild cherries in the Pacific region.

There is even a report of an American Robin feeding on sunflower seeds: Walter M. McKee found a robin feeding and defending one of several sunflower feeders in his yard in Overland Park, Kansas (Vanwoerkom 1996). This possessive robin actually drove other birds, including doves, chickadees, titmice, jays, starlings, cardinals, and grackles, away from the one feeder.

An analysis of stomach contents of more than 1,900 robins, by Nathaniel Wheelwright, included fruit of more than 50 genera and invertebrates of more than 100 families. Diverse diets were found throughout their range. Wheelwright reports that "there was no obvious single feeding niche. The major food classes, consumed in every combination, were soft-bodied invertebrates, hard-bodied invertebrates, and fruit." Beetles and caterpillars were the most important animals; earthworms (difficult to detect soon after ingestion) contributed only 1.5 percent of the animal diet. Other invertebrates often mentioned included ants, cockroaches, cutworms, flies, grasshoppers, millipedes, snails, sowbugs, spiders, and wireworms.

The most important plants consumed, according to Wheelwright, were members of the rose family, especially of the genus *Prunus*, which includes cherries and plums. Cherry eaters will soon "belch" out the undigested seeds. Other berries often eaten by robins included bayberry, blackberry, blueberry, dogwood, greenbrier, hackberry, hawthorn, honeysuckle, juneberry, juniper, madrone, mountain ash, mulberry, poison ivy and poison oak, pokeberry, pyracantha, raspberry, sassafras, serviceberry, spiceberry, sumac, viburnum, and woodbine.

Wheelwright found absolutely no diet difference between males and females. The most interesting result of his study was the "abruptness and magnitude of the shift in diet" from invertebrates to fruit over a one- to two-month period. At the start of the breeding season, less than 10 percent of the robin diet is fruit, but that changes to 90 percent by late summer, even though insects are still plentiful.

In the fall, robins sometimes succumb to the intoxicating effect of certain berries that have become fermented. L. A. Eiserer,

Robin searching for worms. *Photo by John and Gloria Tveten.*

author of *The American Robin: A Backyard Institution,* points out that they "show all the signs of inebriation. They flap, flop, flutter, and stagger. Sometimes they even pass out. But by the next day they will have recovered sufficient sobriety to fly safely away, birdy hangover and all."

Bent includes a description of robin intoxication by Floyd Brallier: "They fall to the ground and lie on their side, occasionally feebly fluttering, apparently as happy as any drunkard in his cups." Oberholser includes this comment: "During some winters in San Antonio and other Texas cities and towns, flocks of these birds gorge on the fruit of Chinaberry, a seminaturalized ornamental tree of Oriental origin. During some years more than others, a few Chinaberries will make a robin tipsy, more will make it drunk, and a big overindulgence will kill the individual. The sight of numerous birds lying about a lawn like Bowery bums seems to amuse some people."

There has been legitimate concern about the robin's effect on commercial fruit crops. Great flocks sometimes invade orchards in the fall. But the benefit resulting from a flock of robins undoubtedly exceeds the amount of fruit eaten. Ornithologist Florence Merriam provides us with the best perspective on this topic: "I have known instances where a Robin who has saved ten to fifteen bushels of apples . . . by clearing the trees of cankerworms in the Spring, was shot when he simply pecked one of the apples that he had saved for the ungrateful fruit-grower."

There also have been numerous reports over the years of American Robins feeding on unusual animal species. Included are trout fry in Massachusetts, stranded fish fry in Yosemite Valley, marine invertebrates along a beach in Rhode Island, white grubs on a Massachusetts cranberry bog, marchflies in an Ohio hayfield, armyworms in a Texas grainfield, flying termites in British Columbia, weevils in cottonfields, butterflies swallowed "wings and all," Japanese beetle larvae dug out of the ground, 17-year locusts on emergence, an eight-inch garter snake, and a dead mouse on Vancouver Island. A snake may stick out of a robin's mouth until it is gradually digested and eventually disappears down the gullet.

In summary, in spring and summer, robins forage mostly on the ground in places where the soil is rich and moist, where earthworms and insects thrive. In fall and winter they feed primarily on berries and other fruit on a wide variety of shrubs, trees, and vines.

Bathing

Few birds bathe so often as American Robins, and from all indications they thoroughly enjoy this activity. My observation of the huge robin flock at Gulf Islands (see Introduction) is perhaps typical. I also have watched two dozen robins gathered around a birdbath waiting their turns while the first contingent of three or four birds splashed and chirped in what seemed like pure contentment. Occasionally a lone robin would appear at my birdbath, as if it had sneaked away from the flock just to bathe without the constraints of others waiting their turns. When alone, they seem to spend a greater amount of time in the bath.

One sunny January afternoon a lone male suddenly appeared on the ground 10 to 12 feet from the birdbath. No other robins were present. Only the typical wintertime feeder birds—Inca Dove, Carolina Chickadee, Tufted Titmouse, Northern Cardinal, Chipping Sparrow, and American Goldfinch—were actively feeding nearby. The robin stood upright and perfectly still for a few seconds and then ran forward a few feet, stopped, and stood alert again, but almost immediately ran to the lip of the birdbath (situated on the ground). It stood there for perhaps 15 seconds, watching for any sign of danger, before it reached down and took a drink. It immediately stood up to swallow the water and repeated this process nine or ten times. Then, with no further hesitation, it stepped forward into the water, where it stood alert again. Almost immediately it began to bathe, dipping its body into the water, with wings drooping down and out, splashing water in every direction. Every few seconds it would pause, stand upright, and check for any possible danger.

Bathing robin. *Photo by Jeffrey Rich.*

It continued its bath, dipping and splashing with all the animation of a Disney character. Twelve times it dipped and splashed, sending water a foot or more in the air. Suddenly, for no apparent reason, it flew up into the live oak tree overhead, where it spent several minutes drying its feathers. Finally, it flew off, probably to join its flock.

I am convinced that our American Robin will bathe twice daily, in the morning and afternoon, whenever the opportunity allows, and it will take advantage of almost every conceivable water. Even rain baths are commonplace; a robin will stand erect in the rain with its bill pointed upward and the water draining off on all sides. It will even droop its wings to expose more of its plumage to the cleansing water. Every now and then robins will shake themselves as if to rid themselves of anything that might be clinging to their feathers. I have seen them bathing in tiny mud puddles following summer rains, in puddles left from watering the lawn, in stock tanks, and in icy streams. Lowell Sumner and Joseph Dixon, in *Birds and Mammals of the Sierra Nevada,* describe robins bathing "in snow water standing along the roadside."

Robins also take dust baths on occasion, although this luxury is far less common than bathing in water. Generally, birds in dry areas dust while those in wet areas bathe. Dusting is simply another method birds use to maintain their feathers. "Experiments with quail show that frequent dusting helps to maintain an optimum amount of oil on the feathers. Excess plumage lipids, including preen oil, are absorbed by the dust and expelled along with dry skin and other debris. Dusting may also help to discourage bird lice" (Ehrlich et al. 1988).

Bent also describes robin sunbaths: "Even on the hottest days, I often see a robin taking a sun bath on my lawn; he crouches on the grass with wings spread, or lies over on one side, with the wing on the sunny side uplifted, so that the sun penetrates under the fluffed-out feathers of the body. It may remain in this position for several minutes, sometimes for many minutes, as if it enjoyed the warmth of the sun, or derived some hygienic benefit from it."

Preening

All birds preen, an act of feather maintenance that generally includes the "nibbling along the feather toward the tip to remove oil, dirt, and ectoparasites . . . or it may simply draw the feather through its partly clamped bill in one movement to smooth the feather barbs and remove dirt from them so that they will lock together" (Terres). It may also include the use of fresh oil from its preen gland (uropygial), located at the base of the tail. The bird rubs its bill and head on the preen oil orifice and then works the oil into the feathers, one at a time.

One preening robin that I watched on a June afternoon in Salt Lake City, Utah, spent about 15 minutes in the act of cleaning what seemed like every feather it could reach. It first fluffed out its body feathers, giving it a larger and rounded appearance. Then, by bending and twisting its neck, it was able to reach every part of its body. It even preened its head feathers by scratching its head with one foot and rubbing its head against the underside of one wing.

Anting

Although the purpose of anting is not well understood, it is performed by more than 200 bird species, including our American Robin. It involves picking up and crushing an ant and rubbing the ant's body fluid on the bird's feathers in a preening fashion. Also, a robin sometimes will sit or lie on an anthill with its feathers fluffed out to allow the ants to swarm up into the feathers. Not all birds of a species ant, suggesting that it is a learned behavior. Some birds seem to have a passion for anting, but others never do it.

Most ornithologists believe that anting is another method of feather maintenance. Ehrlich and colleagues explain that anting "is a way of acquiring the defensive secretions of ants, primarily for their insecticidal, miticidal, fungicidal, or bactericidal properties and, perhaps secondarily, as a supplement to the bird's own preen oil." The ant's formic acid serves to control parasites. Conversely, birds also use harvester ants that have no formic acid.

Birds also have been found anting with a wide variety of additional materials, including mothballs, matches, and cigarette ends. A Jungle Myna was reported anting with a millipede, whose defensive secretions could be smelled 15 feet away.

Flocking and Roosting

A flock of American Robins, scattered across the sky in an irregularly spaced pattern, demonstrates one more of this bird's unique behavioral traits. Like the V pattern of migrating geese, the groupings of American Crows, or the tight flocks of Cedar Waxwings, a flock of robins is so distinct that it can be identified at a considerable distance.

Robin roosting behavior is another distinct trait. Wintering robins congregate at special locations each evening, often by the thousands. These areas, which may be as large as one square mile, are extremely noisy places with much singing and calling. By late winter, birds may be in full song. Feeding areas may be spread out over a 12-mile radius. Spring and summer roosts are dominated by male robins; females remain on the nests. By autumn, the roosts contain both the males and females, as well as all the young of the year and even occasional migrants. The resident birds occupy these roosts until migration.

Life History

AN American Robin that survives beyond the nest to adulthood has a life expectancy of 10 years, although when nestling deaths are included in data from bird-banding recoveries, the average drops to only 1 year and 2 months. A robin's maximum recorded lifespan is 17 years, according to Terres: "a captive Robin at Tarrytown, N.Y., lived for 17 years; another, at Richmond, Ore., [was] alive and healthy at 17." In comparison, maximum known ages for some other birds range from 9 years for the Mourning Dove, 11 years for the Dark-eyed Junco, 14 years for the Peregrine Falcon, 20 years for the Mallard, 23 years for the Canada Goose, and 24 years for the Common Raven.

Donald Farner reports the "age-group composition" of the 855 robins within his study as 53 percent first-year birds, 25 percent second-year birds, less than 14 percent third-year birds, less than 6 percent fourth-year birds, less than 2 percent fifth-year birds, and less than 1 percent birds six years and older.

It is estimated that a pair of adult American Robins potentially can produce 100 offspring during a 10-year lifetime. Eiserer points out that if there were no mortality, a pair of robins has the potential to produce "19.5 million descendants by the end of their ten-year lifespan! . . . At the end of a mere thirty years, the original pair of Robins would have 1.2 billion trillion descendants!" Robins, however, like all wild birds, experience a high mortality rate.

Reproduction is the essential purpose of a robin's existence. The breeding cycle itself includes seven distinct parts: migration, territory, courtship, nest building, egg laying, incubation, and care of the young.

American Robin, Turdus migratorius. *Photo by Ro Wauer.*

Migration

The first urge to breed undoubtedly occurs on a bird's wintering grounds. Although ornithologists do not agree on which of the external factors—including the length of day, temperature, rainfall, and food abundance—is the key triggering mechanism, the increased hours of daylight, at least for northern wintering birds, seems to be extremely important.

Spring migration is clearly the first step in a bird's breeding cycle; it must get from its winter home to the location where it is to nest. Northbound American Robins are one of the few bird species that migrate by both day and night. These travelers generally keep pace with the advance of spring. Collins and Boyajians report that the robin's northward movement "follows the 37 degree F isotherms, averaging about 38 miles a day." Isotherms are the invisible latitude lines tracing areas on the earth's surface generally having the same temperature at a given time.

In the warmer southern states, robin migration can begin very early in the new year. Tyler describes an enormous flight of robins that a Mr. Knowlton reported for Florida on February 14, 15, and 16: "They came from a southern direction, and were continuing passing, alighting and repassing. . . . The air was full of them, and their numbers beyond estimate, reminded him of bees. Mr. Knowlton heard that this movement of Robins had been noted for a distance of ten miles away, across the flight."

At Cape May, New Jersey, Witmer Stone reported that the earliest northward robin movements there usually were detected between February 25 and March 16, but some years this initial movement did not occur until early April. Also from the Northeast, Tyler describes a "typical" robin arrival in Massachusetts on the morning of March 15:

> Looking southward across a broad meadow, we saw them coming toward us, the first we had seen, a flock of a dozen or more, flying in open order, but rather evenly spaced, not closely packed like blackbirds. When they came to the northern edge of the

meadow and caught sight of a patch of greensward, they checked
their flight and settled on the grass. . . . All through the day,
spent between Boston and Newburyport, the robin was a promi-
nent bird, chiefly during the morning hours, mostly in small
flocks, but sometimes collected in dozens, spread over the open
fields.

In South Texas, wintering birds normally leave in March, although a few individuals may linger to early May. At my home
in Victoria, Texas, all of the wintering robins generally move out
by late March, although small passing flocks can be expected
through mid-April. In California, Bent reports "large flocks migrating over Pasadena flying high and headed northward" on
February 11, and on March 6 and 7, "large numbers of robins
gathered in the camphortrees in front of my house; the trees
were fairly alive with them. Others were seen flying about in
loose flocks and were probably migrants."

Bent includes numerous spring arrival dates for locations all
across the continent. These provide further insight into the
robin's northward migration. A sample includes: Omaha, Nebraska, February 10; Denver, Colorado, February 16; Chicago,
Illinois, February 21; Washington, D.C., February 25; Grand Rap-
ids, Michigan, March 3; Stockbridge, Massachusetts, March 10;
Yellowstone National Park, Wyoming, March 11; Machias,
Maine, March 14; Banff, Alberta, March 25; St. John's, Newfoundland, April 6; Dawson, Yukon, May 9; Kobuk River,
Alaska, May 20.

The spring arrival of the American Robin provides many
northern dwellers an emotional uplift. The first spring robins
are most welcome to residents in all the northern states and
provinces. Merriam writes, "When they come back what good
cheer they bring with them! I remember one long winter spent
in the country when it seemed that spring would never come.
At last one day the call of a Robin rang out, and on one of the
few bare spots made by the melting snow there stood the first
redbreast! It was a sight I can never forget, for the intense delight of such moments make bright spots in a lifetime."

A robin flock settled on the ground.
Photo by Maslowski Wildlife Productions.

Herbert Brandt describes a similar scene: "Over much of its range, no other bird casts a charm like the robin. It is the harbinger of spring; while ice and snow may still bind the landscape and the frost crunch underfoot, the early coming of the robin is usually the accepted sign that the stern reign of King Winter is on the wane. Then happiness fills the hearts of the multitude, for spring soon will be here."

Territory and Territorial Defense

Nest-site fidelity for American Robins is much greater than it is for wintering sites. Farner discovered that at least 70 percent of young banded robins in Washington state returned the next year to within 25 miles of their birthplace. In Iowa, Joseph Hickey found that of 61 banded robins, "about half of the first generation returned to nest in the region of their birthplace, about a fifth nested within 10 miles, while the remainder scattered, even up to a distance of 400 miles away" (Collins and Boyajians). Nationwide, banding returns indicate that about 74 percent of robins return to within 10 miles of their birthplace.

Male robins arrive on their breeding territory before the females, and Brandt provides us with his perspective on that arrival:

> Mr. Robin arrives during the night and takes his station on a cold, naked limb on a tree top overlooking his chosen territory. . . . For two or three days, perhaps a bit longer, he sits about, or searches for food. If the weather is cold or stormy, he huddles up in his fluffy garments of red, never uttering a shaft of song, although he may "put! put!" in his own style when disturbed by a cat or squirrel. Then on another morning, there is a paler mate; she evidently arrived likewise during the hours of darkness. Over her he makes no ado whatsoever, but merely accepts her coming as a prearranged matter of course. He apparently did nothing after his arrival to entice her back to their old trysting-place. She, too, knew the exact pinpoint whereon to land at the end of her extended night migration.

More often than not, the older experienced males are the first to arrive and claim nesting territories. The inexperienced males usually must settle for secondary sites. The size of the nesting territory, the place where mating and nesting occurs, may range from one-third to three-quarters of an acre, although the territory is usually less than half an acre, smaller than that of most other birds of equal size. A few examples include the Red-winged Blackbird (about 0.7 acre), Northern Mockingbird (0.1 to 1.5 acres), Red-eyed Vireo (1.4 to 2.1 acres), Hairy Woodpecker (6 to 8 acres), and Eastern and Western meadowlarks (3 to 15 acres).

Males generally select the breeding territory, which they defend with their mate until fall, while sharing common feeding grounds on lawns, golf courses, cemeteries, pastures, and the like. A robin's nesting territory, therefore, is more fluid than that of most other songbirds, perhaps because of the shared feeding grounds. Their breeding territories often overlap, so there are instances when their territories are not strongly defended. As a general rule, robins are more aggressive toward other robins in the vicinity of their nests than they are outside the immediate area. The amount of aggression declines as the distance from the nest increases.

Robins from nearby territories will often join their neighbors in defending a nest site. Joseph Howell reports that when examining nests, he was often "scolded by four or five Robins, and once by as many as twelve." He adds, "As long as the security of the nest is not threatened, the owners make no attempts, or only half-hearted endeavors, to force other Robins from the territory. Once the cause of the alarm has disappeared the Robins, excepting the parents, depart peaceably."

Eiserer points out that a robin's territorial defense is most effective in the center of its territory: "Robins win over 80 percent of the disputes occurring in the middle of their properties, compared to 60 percent at the territorial boundaries and only 30 percent a hundred yards beyond those boundaries." Eiserer also suggests that the female robin is more effective than the male, winning 75 percent of her battles, slightly more than the 70-percent win ratio of the male.

Territorial defense may range from simple posturing, such as a casual lift into the air, to an aggressive chase with much scolding and shrieking. Who has not watched a noisy robin chase, with one male in hot pursuit of another? At other times, a male may simply run at another, both jumping in the air like two gamecocks. There are numerous records of territorial robins attacking their own image in a windowpane or mirror.

Stokes divides territorial posturing into four categories. The "attack-run" involves one bird, with its body low to the ground, running at another. The "tail-lift" involves the bird lowering its head and lifting its tail while facing an opponent. The "crouch," often preceding an attack, is given when another bird approaches too close. "Pushing" is "a more subtle form of aggression where one bird simply keeps taking short runs toward another bird and the other bird keeps moving slightly away from it, making its own short runs."

More aggressive defensive actions are often exhibited against predators and other assumedly deadly adversaries. There are numerous examples of robins attacking considerably larger wildlife. Hawks, owls, jays, crows, grackles, squirrels, cats, and dogs receive equal treatment. A pair of American Robins actually killed a Steller's Jay by pummeling it with numerous vicious blows.

Nest predators will often be mobbed by the nearest nesting robins along with several of their neighbors simply for passing too near an active nest. The defenders may dive at the intruder, sometimes striking it on its back, snapping their beaks, and making loud clicking sounds.

Even snakes are the object of a robin's wrath when they get too close to a nest. Northern brown, garter, and ribbon snakes have all been killed by attacking robins.

Territorial defense is not always limited to wildlife. R. D. Lawrence describes an incident in which he personally was attacked by a territorial robin:

While I was lounging in the spring sunshine, I was startled by the swoop of a male robin, who had been sitting in a tree watching me as he sang loudly. Suddenly the bird hurled himself from his perch and flew straight for my head, turning away only when I ducked instinctively. He landed on another tree and resumed his singing and I settled once more to watch. Again he flew at me, this time actually hitting my cap. It was then that I remembered that my headpiece was robin-breast orange. The bird took my hat for a rival! After he had flown at me for a third time, I took off the cap and propped it in a small pin cherry tree. Then stepped away to watch. Almost at once the robin flew at the cap and began to peck it and claw at it, twittering furiously at the same time, and the "battle" only ended when the cap fell to the ground and landed upside down, showing the white lining. The attacker, evidently believing that he had routed his rival, returned to his first perch and began to sing.

Courtship

The arrival of the female bird normally signifies the start of courtship. Typical of most songbirds, our American Robin is almost always monogamous, having only one mate at a time. But there are a few records of a male robin with a new mate with each clutch, or rarely with more than one mate all during the breeding season. There also are cases of the female mate of the previous year arriving to find her place already taken; she then drives the interloper away.

A monogamous pairing does not mean that the birds are mated for life, as the mating relationship continues only through the nesting season. However, both sexes generally return to the same territory the following year and therefore are likely to mate for a second or more times. Conversely, banding studies have shown that although the female may return to the previous year's territory, she may not always breed with the same mate.

Courtship itself varies with the beholder. The majority of descriptions of robin courtship undoubtedly are largely influenced by the writer's own romanticism. Don C. Trenary provides us with his perspective on American Robin courtship:

> The wooing of the Robin is a disappointment to believers in romance. There are no grotesque dances, such as highlight the courtship of many bird species; no fights over females, no song that is exclusively a mating call. In the practical mind of the male Robin, a choice of territory looms far more important than a choice of mate. Under such haphazard arrangements, a Robin may get together with the mate he had the previous summer. Then again, he may not.

John James Audubon's description of robin courtship is quoted by Bent as follows:

> During the pairing season, the male pays his address to the female of his choice frequently on the ground, and with a fervor evincing the strongest attachment. I have often seen him, at the earliest dawn of a May morning, strutting around her with all the pomposity of a pigeon. Sometimes along a space of ten or twelve yards, he is seen with his tail fully spread, his wings shaking, and his throat inflated, running over the grass and brushing it, as it were, until he has neared his mate, when he moves round her several times without once rising from the ground. She then receives his caresses.

Bent also includes a very different perspective on robin courtship by Bradford Torrey:

> How gently he approaches his beloved! How carefully he avoids ever coming disrespectfully near! No sparrow-like screaming, no dancing about, no melodramatic gesticulation. If she moves from one side of the tree to the other, or to the tree adjoining, he follows in silence. Yet every movement is a petition, an assurance that his heart is hers and ever must be. . . . On one occasion, at least, I saw him holding himself absolutely motionless, in a horizontal posture, staring at his sweetheart as if he would charm her with his gaze, and emitting all the while a

subdued hissing sound. The significance of this conduct I do not profess to have understood; it ended with his suddenly darting at the female, who took wing and was pursued.

Nest Building

The robin's nesting activity involves a rapid increase to a peak and then a slow decline. Although the exact time of nesting varies throughout the continent, nesting generally begins in mid-April, peaks by late April, gradually declines through mid-June, and continues a slow decline through July. In Illinois, an area that might represent the mean, the nesting cycle requires a total of 27 to 38 days: 3 to 10 days for nest building, 11 to 13 days for incubation, and 13 to 15 days of nestling life.

The incredible variety of nesting locations inhabited by American Robins illustrates the adaptability of this bird more than almost any other facet of its behavior. It also is directly related to its expanded range, evidence of the robin's ability to survive in a changing environment.

Robin nest sites range from ground level, on Gardener's Island, New York, "in the absence of mammalian predators" (Collias and Collias 1984), to the upper canopy of trees, always in a sheltered location, and on a firm support such as a tree fork or crotch. At Jasper National Park, Canada, I discovered a robin nest with four eggs 2.5 feet above the ground in a 4-foot-tall fir tree on June 12.

Early nests are often placed in evergreens because of the dense cover these trees provide during the early season, but later nests are more often placed in deciduous trees that are then fully leaved. Howell calculates that in New York, 69 percent of 49 first nests were located in evergreens, whereas only 44 percent of 52 later nests were located in evergreens. He also reports that the "geometric mean" nest was at a height of 16.4 feet. A similar study in Michigan revealed nest heights ranging from less than 1 foot to as much as 66 feet with an average height of 10.2 feet. Bent reports a nest "in the midst of an elevated mass of sphagnum."

Robin collecting mud for its nest. *Photo by Tom J. Ulrich.*

Additional natural nest sites include the unused nests of several other animals, including Mourning Doves, Eastern Phoebes, Gray Catbirds, Common Grackles, orioles, squirrels, and hornets. Robins occasionally will nest in close association with other bird species. They have constructed nests on top of nesting boxes being used by Tree Swallows, Eastern Bluebirds, and House Wrens. Morse reports a Wisconsin robin nest only 14 inches from a nest of an Eastern Kingbird. Wetherbee found a robin nest in a clump of lilacs a few feet above a Gray Catbird nest, and the robin even helped incubate the catbird eggs and feed the young. Bailey and Niedrak report that a single "community nest" contained four half-grown robins and four eggs and two very young House Finch nestlings; both species fed the nestlings. Raney reports that a robin and a Mourning Dove shared the same nest, alternately incubating the eggs and feeding the young.

Robin nests have also been found in an amazing assortment of human-made structures. Examples include the top of a fence post, clothesline post, and gate post; on a rail fence, wheel hub, smoke pipe, tire iron, window ledge, fire escape step, gutter, lamp bracket, porch railing, barn, shed, outhouse, and telephone booth; on top of a birdhouse; on a fish-drying rack; in the pocket of a coat left hanging on a tree; on the stone base of a cemetery monument; and inside an eel trap. But the following nesting sites are truly unique.

John Burroughs, in *The Summit of the Years,* reports a pair of robins building their nest under the box of the running gear of a farmer's wagon. He writes that "the farmer was in the habit of making two trips to the village two miles away each week. The Robins followed him on those trips, and the mother bird went forward with her incubation while the farmer did his errands, and the birds returned with him when he drove home. And strange to say, the brood was duly hatched and reproduced."

An Ohio robin "began 26 separate nests in the spaces between a wooden girder and the roof rafters lying across it," according to Eiserer. "After a week of self-indulgence among

A robin's nest built on a tombstone. *Photo by Tom J. Ulrich.*

these irresistible sites, with workmen supplying building materials and placing bets on where the final functional nest would be, the female settled on one nest, laid eggs, and hatched them."

In Michigan, robins built a nest on the arm of an active oil well pump. They raised a brood as the arm rose and fell with each stroke. At Sioux City, Iowa, robins built their nest on a locomotive that went to and from Chicago. The female completed her nesting chores by following the train along its journey.

The final decision on the nest site is pretty much up to the female. Yet some female robins have a difficult time making up their mind and may start two or more nests before settling on a single site. Experienced females, however, might simply repair an old nest or build a new one on the old foundation. As many as six nests have been built on top of another.

Nest construction is done primarily by the female robin, although her mate assists by bringing her nest materials. When building a nest, both sexes can often be found with huge loads of nest materials. One female robin at Curecanti National Recreation Area, Colorado, was so loaded down that her package of twigs and grass doubled her head size; she looked like a flying ball of litter.

Robins are opportunists when it comes to selecting nest building materials, utilizing almost everything they come upon. Twigs and grasses dominate the list of materials used by southern birds, but mosses and lichens are the most likely ingredients in northern nests. H. W. Henshaw, the author of the ornithological chapter in an 1875 U.S. Army publication, *Report upon Geographical and Geological Explorations and Surveys West of the One Hundredth Meridian*, states that in sheep country they found robin nests "composed almost wholly of wool." More typical secondary nesting materials include weed stalks, pine needles, feathers, string, bits of cloth, and mammal hair.

Richard Headstrom, author of *A Complete Field Guide to Nests in the United States*, provides us with a general description of a robin nest: "Cup-shaped, thick-walled, bulky, sometimes

rough appearing and unkempt; of coarse grasses, twigs, rootlets, paper, cloth, and string, with an inner wall of mud; lined
usually with fine grasses. Outside diameter, about 6½ inches;
outside height, about 3 inches; inside diameter, 4 inches; inside
depth, 2½ inches." Mud is an essential ingredient in every robin
nest. It is used to cement the nest materials in place. The female
robin carries gummy mud pellets in her bill, sometimes from a
distance of a quarter-mile away. She uses her breast to shape,
smooth, and pack the mud into the nest. Nicholas and Elsie
Collias point out that "American Robin nests contain more
mud when the birds have to use short material, more tough
flexible rootlets when the nest is in an especially windy spot, and
more moss when in a relatively cold microclimate."

Collins and Boyajians assert that if "the weather is dry, the
bird may take dirt in its bill and wet it in water, or take water in
its bill to bring in to moisten the dry dirt." Eiserer describes a
female that immersed itself in a birdbath "and then shook herself off in a nearby dusty road." Another female reversed the
process: "she scooped dirt into her mouth and then dipped her
bill in water before continuing nestward." Alice Ball writes of a
clever robin that waded in a birdbath, then hopped into the
dust, and with her bill scraped the mud off her legs. She did this
repeatedly until she had the necessary amount.

Eiserer describes the robin's nest construction as consisting
of three stages: (1) firm foundation of "course grass, straw, rootlets, and occasionally pieces of paper or rags" molded by the
female; (2) inner lining of mud one-quarter to one inch thick,
situated to shape the nest; and (3) fine, soft grasses placed into
the moist mud to form the inner cup.

Nest construction normally takes 4 or 6 days but can take up
to 20 days in bad weather. But if the nest is destroyed, the female may rebuild it in a single day.

Later broods may be raised in the same refurbished nest, or
the female may complete a second nearby nest in 2 or 3 days.
More than half of the second broods are raised in nests built at
a new location.

Robin nest and eggs. *Photo by John and Gloria Tveten.*

Egg-Laying

Egg-laying may begin immediately or may be postponed a few days after nest completion. Egg-laying usually occurs in the early morning hours, one each day until the set is complete.

The normal robin egg complement is four eggs, although sometimes the set is limited to three and rarely grows to five, six, or even seven eggs. Collins and Boyajians claim that four eggs is typical in the East and South, but three seems "to be the common number in the West, the Arctic, and Newfoundland." In Illinois, Graber and colleagues found 74 percent of all first nests contained four eggs and 23 percent contained three eggs. In June and July, however, only 46 percent contained four eggs and 48 percent contained three eggs. Five eggs were found in less than 4 percent of all clutches, and six or seven eggs occurred in less than 1 percent of all nests.

The typical robin egg is robin's-egg blue, a pastel blue, but freshly laid eggs may be greenish or (rarely) spotted with dark or dull brown. Most possess a dull or slight luster but become glossy after being incubated a few days. Of 50 American Robin eggs in the National Museum, measurements ranged from 31.6 to 23.8 millimeters in length and 20.3 to 16.8 millimeters across (or 1.2 to 0.9 inches long by 0.8 to 0.7 inch wide).

Incubation

Incubation normally begins during the evening after the second egg is laid and lasts for 11 to 14 days, with an average of about 13 days. The entire incubation process is usually done by the female. She may sit on the nest 60 to 80 percent of the daytime hours, depending on the weather. Even in good weather she rarely leaves for more than 5 to 10 minutes at a time. She is fully responsible for maintaining the proper incubation temperature, keeping the eggs warm during cold weather and shaded during extremely hot weather. She also must turn or rotate the eggs several times daily. This is done by hopping on the rim of the nest and gently rolling the eggs with her bill. Egg turning helps keep all the eggs at a uniform temperature and prevents the embryos from sticking to the inside of the eggshells.

Male robins remain in the vicinity throughout the daylight hours and will respond immediately if the female gives a call of alarm. A male may even bring food to feed his mate; however, more often than not she will leave the nest to feed herself. Males only occasionally sit on the eggs.

Hatching may take an entire day; each chick must fight its way out of the egg, first by breaking a hole in the shell with its egg tooth, a hard protrusion on its beak, and then struggling mightily, between periods of rest, for its release. Most often the eggs will hatch a day apart in the order they were laid. Lower or warmer than normal incubation temperatures can extend or reduce incubation times.

Care of the Young

Care of the young robins, which are unable at first to do anything but lift their head and open their mouth for food, begins as soon as the eggs hatch. Although naked, reddish, wet, and blind, a nestling's high body temperature, rapid heart beat and circulation, and rapid digestion, growth, and metabolism require large quantities of food. And so, after the eggs hatch, the parent's responsibilities change dramatically from incubating eggs and providing nest security to finding food and feeding the clamoring youngsters. Both parents participate fully in these time-consuming chores.

For the first four days of a nestling's existence it is fed by regurgitation. The food is first swallowed by the parent birds, who then regurgitate the partly digested food into the bright orange, yawning gapes of the nestlings. By their fifth day, the nestlings are receiving earthworms that have been broken into small mouthfuls. As the days go by, complete worms and large insects are given to the growing youngsters.

Collins and Boyajians claim that during a two-week nest life, a brood of robins "will eat 3.2 pounds of food." Further, by "the last day in the nest, a young Robin may eat 14 feet of

Male robin feeding young with the female looking on.
Photo by Jeffrey Rich.

earthworms." How can the parents possibly keep up with their hungry brood? It requires every waking hour, and in the northern latitudes feeding time may extend to 21 hours a day. Although the robin's average nest life may be 13 days, including an average of 100 feeding visits every day, at Aumiu, Alaska, the nest life lasts only 9 days but includes 137 feeding visits each day.

Although earthworms are an essential part of the nestlings' diet, they are not their principal food. Fred Charles found that Illinois robins put in 15.5 hours day feeding young in late May, bringing an average of 356 pieces of food daily. "Lepidoptera larvae [caterpillars] composed about 50 percent of the total food, with earthworms (about 29 percent), ants (about 7 percent), Diptera [flies] (about 6 percent), and small percentages of Coleoptera [beetles], Myriapoda [centipedes and millipedes], and adult Lepidoptera [butterflies and moths] making up most of the other half."

The nestlings undergo a remarkably rapid development. Roger Pasquier, in *Watching Birds: An Introduction to Ornithology*, points out that robins experience a 1000-percent growth rate in 10 days. They are "born weighing 5.5 grams, and leave the nest 13 days later weighing 56 grams." Baby robins open their eyes on the sixth day after hatching and also are able to grasp objects actively with their mandibles. By the eighth day the youngsters are fully feathered, except on the stomach, and their body is able to maintain a temperature of about 109 degrees F. By day 10 or 11, the larger, more aggressive youngsters are capable of leaving the nest. Except for their speckled breast, stubby tail, and a few remaining pin feathers here and there, they look very much like their parents.

During the first few days of nest life the nestlings are extremely vulnerable to dangers from outside the nest, from predators to weather that can be too cold, too hot, too windy, or too wet. The summer sun can easily kill newly hatched robins within 15 to 20 minutes if they are not shaded by the female. She may actually bring water in her bill to cool the nestlings. Edward Forbush, in *Birds of Massachusetts and Other New England States*, describes how one set of parents protected their young during a particularly bad summer rainstorm: They "perched on opposite sides of the nest, breasts pressed together and heads crossed by each other, their bodies and wings thus sheltering their young like a pitched roof, while the rain ran harmlessly off on both sides."

Nest maintenance is extremely important from egg-laying through fledging. After the eggs hatch, the adults carry shell remains away, dropping them at a distance so they do not attract predators. Nestling excrement (fecal sacs) is also carefully removed and either dropped elsewhere or swallowed. Since nestlings normally defecate after each feeding, the adults develop a habit of bringing in food and taking away the fecal sacs.

The adults also remove any foreign objects found in the nest. One parent fed a nestling a piece of meat too large for the nestling to swallow immediately. The parent then followed the instinct for nest maintenance and carried away the piece of meat with the baby bird attached. It was a perfect example of throwing the baby out with the bathwater.

As soon as the young fledge or leave the nest, the male robin takes full responsibility for feeding and protecting them. This allows the female to begin a second brood, which may begin within a week after the first brood is fledged.

The youngsters normally leave the nest one at a time, depending on their age, but a sudden disturbance at the nest can cause a mass exodus, a "flapping explosion of plump and chirping cannonballs that scatter in all directions," as Eiserer describes it. The parents must then feed the babies on the ground or wherever they land. Once out of the nest they rarely return, and their inability to detect danger or care for themselves often leads to disaster. House cats are the baby bird's greatest danger; house cat depredation is discussed further in the section Enemies and Threats.

During this extremely vulnerable period, however, a baby bird, in or out of the nest, may receive food from a number of other parent birds, robins as well as various other species. There are records of Song Sparrows feeding baby robins and also cleaning the nest. Gabrielson and Jewett report that a Swainson's Thrush in Oregon "repeatedly fed young fledgling robins, voluntary assistance probably greatly appreciated by the hardworking parents." Eastern Bluebirds were found defending baby robins from a Blue Jay attack, and an adult robin was observed feeding a baby chicken, trying to force food down its throat.

George M. Sutton, in *Birds Worth Watching*, provides us with the following description of the robin's postnesting activities: "The old birds feed the young for several days after the brood leaves the nest, but force them to be 'on their own' about the time their tails reach full length. It is amusing to see a parent, worn out with feeding a young one, refuse to put the food into the gaping mouth but drop it in the grass instead. 'Go ahead. Pick it up. It's time for you to be finding your own food' the old bird seems to be saying."

Another interesting description of fledgling birds comes from Bent, who paraphrases James Russell Lowell. The postnesting fledglings are described as "plump innocent-looking birds with spotted breasts and stumpy tails, staring up at the sky with little sign of fear, a choice morsel for the house cat." Bent adds:

> They soon become wary, however, and before long are able
> to avoid attack by running swiftly away, or flying out of reach.
> The male parents now take full charge of the broods, and as they
> scud over the grass plots in search of earthworms, the little birds
> follow them about expectantly, waiting for them to pull out the
> worms, shake them, and thrust them into their throats. The
> fledglings rapidly acquire the manner of adult birds. In a few
> days they throw off the crouching attitude of the nestling and
> assume the erect, proud bearing of adult birds, and in less than
> two weeks are able, but not always willing, to find food for
> themselves. The male parent is thus free to aid in the care of
> the next brood, which is almost ready to hatch.

All during the initial nesting cycle males continue to fly to a communal roost every night after delivering their evening songs. Once the first brood is fledged and able to fly, the youngsters join the adult males. As soon as the last brood is flying, the females and all the birds of the year also join the robin assemblages. A few other bird species, including kingbirds, Brown Thrashers, Cedar Waxwings, Red-winged Blackbirds, Common Grackles, and orioles, may also join the roosting robins. These same birds may occupy the communal roost until departing on their fall migration.

Associates

There is an old adage that you can tell a great deal about someone from the company he or she keeps. This may also be true for birds, at least while nesting. Robin associates, the various other birds that share the immediate vicinity of their nesting sites, vary across the continent. These associates also provide a different perspective on the communities in which our American Robins live. The following examples, representing a variety of habitats, were derived from the 1983 breeding bird censuses, all published in *American Birds*.

On a 10.6-acre study site in a suburban bird sanctuary in Nassau County, New York, dominated by a deciduous forest of red maples, tulip trees, and other species, Marguerite Wolffsohn and William J. Kolodnicki recorded 62 territorial male birds of 26 species. Along with 3 breeding pairs of the American Robin, they also found Gray Catbird (10.5 pairs), Northern Cardinal (10 pairs), Common Grackle (7.5 pairs), House Wren (7 pairs), Baltimore Oriole (3 pairs), Blue Jay (2.5 pairs), Black-capped Chickadee (2.5 pairs), Downy Woodpecker (2 pairs), Wood Thrush (1.5 pairs), Mourning Dove, Yellow-billed Cuckoo, Red-bellied Woodpecker, Northern Flicker, Tufted Titmouse, White-breasted Nuthatch, European Starling, Red-eyed Vireo, Song Sparrow, House Finch (each with 1 pair), and Eastern Screech-Owl, Hairy Woodpecker, American Crow, Veery, Scarlet Tanager, and House Sparrow (each with less than 1 pair).

On a 100-acre tract of abandoned farmland in Champaign County, Illinois, David J. Tazik recorded 111 territorial males of 29 species. Along with 3 breeding pairs of the American Robin, he also found Common Yellowthroat and Red-winged Blackbird (both with 15 pairs), Field Sparrow (11 pairs), Willow Flycatcher, Yellow Warbler, Yellow-breasted Chat (each with 8 pairs), Northern Cardinal, Indigo Bunting (each with 6 pairs), Brown Thrasher (5 pairs), Gray Catbird (4 pairs), Ring-necked Pheasant, House Wren, Bell's Vireo, Eastern Towhee (each with 3 pairs), Mourning Dove, Yellow-billed Cuckoo, Song Sparrow (each with 2 pairs), Green Heron, Ruby-throated Hummingbird, White-eyed Vireo, Rose-breasted Grosbeak (each with 1 pair), and Downy Woodpecker, Eastern Kingbird, Blue Jay, European Starling, Common Grackle, Brown-headed Cowbird, and American Goldfinch (each with less than 1 pair).

On a 37-acre suburban cemetery in Jefferson County, Alabama, Thomas A. Imhof recorded 95 territorial males of 25 species. Along with 12 American Robins, he recorded European Starling (13 pairs), House Sparrow (12 pairs), Northern Mockingbird (9 pairs), Blue Jay, Northern Cardinal (both with 8 pairs), Mourning Dove, Eastern Towhee (both with 5 pairs), Common Grackle (4 pairs), Brown Thrasher, Brown-headed Cowbird (both with 3 pairs), Rock Dove (2 pairs), Red-bellied and Downy woodpeckers, Northern Flicker, Great Crested Flycatcher, Carolina Chickadee, Tufted Titmouse, Carolina Wren, Wood Thrush, Northern Parula, Red-winged Blackbird, House Finch (each with 1 pair), and Chimney Swift, and Eastern Meadowlark (each with less than 1 pair).

On an 18.6-acre forest of Douglas fir and ponderosa pine in El Paso County, Colorado, Don Van Horn recorded 31.5 territorial males or females of 17 species. Along with 4 breeding pairs of the American Robin, he also found Spotted Towhee (8 pairs), Black-billed Magpie (6 pairs), Black-capped Chickadee (3 pairs), Virginia's Warbler (2.5 pairs), White-breasted Nuthatch (2 pairs), Mourning Dove, Northern Flicker, Western Scrub-Jay, Brown-headed Cowbird, Bullock's Oriole (each with 1 pair), and Black-headed Grosbeak, Brewer's Blackbird, Downy Woodpecker, American Crow, European Starling, and Chipping Sparrow (each with less than 1 pair).

On a 25-acre campground in old orchards in Washington

County, Utah, Jerome Gifford recorded 87 territorial males of 15 species. Along with 19 pairs of the American Robin, he also found House Sparrow (12 pairs), Black-headed Grosbeak, Bullock's Oriole (both with 8 pairs), Black-chinned Hummingbird, European Starling (both with 7 pairs), Solitary Vireo, Yellow Warbler (both with 5 pairs), Warbling Vireo, Brown-headed Cowbird, Lesser Goldfinch (all with 3 pairs), Mourning Dove (2 pairs), Hairy Woodpecker (1 pair), and Western Wood-Pewee and Black Phoebe (both with less than 1 pair).

On 80 acres of scattered mixed coniferous forest in subalpine meadows and spruce bogs in Grant County, Oregon, Robert A. Hudson recorded 47 territorial males of 11 species. Along with 4 pairs of the American Robin, he also found Chipping Sparrow (13 pairs), Cassin's Finch (9 pairs), Ruby-crowned Kinglet, White-crowned Sparrow (both with 5 pairs), Yellow-rumped Warbler, Dark-eyed Junco (both with 3 pairs), Fox Sparrow (2 pairs), and Spotted Sandpiper, Mountain Bluebird, and Varied Thrush (each with 1 pair).

On a 20.9-acre mature forest of pine and fir in Nevada County, California, Michael P. Yoder-Williams and Kimberly With recorded 28 territorial males of 18 species. Along with 1 pair of the American Robin, they recorded Golden-crowned Kinglet (3.5 pairs), Yellow-rumped Warbler, Dark-eyed Junco (both with 3 pairs), *Empidonax* flycatchers, Mountain Chickadee (both with 2.5 pairs), Red-breasted Nuthatch, Hermit Thrush, Western Tanager (all with 2 pairs), Brown Creeper, Townsend's Solitaire (both with 1.5 pairs), Northern Flicker, Steller's Jay, Evening Grosbeak (each with 1 pair), and Calliope Hummingbird, Hairy Woodpecker, Red Crossbill, and Pine Siskin (each with less than 1 pair).

Enemies and Threats

P REDATORS, competitors, cowbirds, overindulgence, weather, diseases, and a few human activities are persistent dangers to American Robins. In spite of their enemies and threats, robins are more abundant today than any time in the past. They possess an amazing ability to exploit vacant niches and overcome the abundant losses from their enemies and threats.

Predators

Our American Robin must be ever alert to the varied and abundant predators that it encounters daily. Raptors are constantly present on its breeding and wintering grounds, as well as along its migration routes. Robins are more susceptible to raptors than many other songbirds because of their habit of flying out in the open, commonly crossing open country. Sharp-shinned Hawks, for instance, although not much larger than the robin, are almost always present. They follow their prey year-round, from their summer homes to their wintering grounds and back again. They can strike at any place and at any time during the day. At night there are a number of owls that can take a poorly hidden robin.

The following raptors are known to prey on American Robins: Northern Harrier, Sharp-shinned Hawk, Cooper's Hawk, Northern Goshawk, Gyrfalcon, Red-shouldered Hawk, Broadwinged Hawk, Red-tailed Hawk, American Kestrel, Merlin, Peregrine Falcon, Eastern Screech-Owl, Western Screech-Owl, Great Horned Owl, Northern Pygmy-Owl, Snowy Owl, Long-eared Owl, Barred Owl, and Northern Saw-whet Owl.

The accipiters—especially Sharp-shinned and Cooper's hawks —are known as bird hawks because they so often prey on other

Great Horned Owl and robin.
Photo by Maslowski Wildlife Productions.

birds. Of more than 1,000 Sharp-shinned Hawk stomachs examined, "only 64 did not contain bird remains," according to Alexander Sprunt, Jr., in *North American Birds of Prey.* He further reports that 224 of 422 Cooper's Hawk stomachs contained birds.

In the northern forests, the Merlin is one of the most effective bird hawks. According to Tom Doolittle's master's thesis on Merlins at Voyageurs National Park, Minnesota, a pair of Merlins will take 550 songbirds, including robins, each nesting season.

John Burroughs also documented the attack of a Loggerhead Shrike. In a 1913 essay he writes:

> Late in the winter, while trimming the grapevines, I heard a bird scream, and, looking in the direction, saw that a robin was being hotly pursued by a shrike. The robin was darting in and about a spruce-tree, screaming his protest and leaving a trail of feathers behind where the shrike struck him. Presently, still shouting his protests, he left the shelter of the spruces and disappeared over the hill, closely pursued by the shrike. What the final issue was no one knows. I had not supposed that the shrike ever attacked so large a bird as the robin. He certainly could not carry away a bird of more than his own weight, though he might kill it by a blow upon its head, as he probably did in this case.

Besides the direct threats from predators, there also are reports of Steller's Jays, Blue Jays, Western Scrub Jays, Gray Jays, American Crows, Common Ravens, and Common and Great-tailed grackles robbing robin nests and carrying away nestlings. Snakes are especially dangerous during the summer months. Blacksnakes have been seen taking young and adults, and Harold B. Wood observed a robin being strangled by a Smooth Green Snake: "The snake was wound so tightly around the bird's neck, by four complete turns, that it could not be shaken loose" (Bent 1964).

Mammals also are a factor in robin predation. Raccoons, bobcats, black bears, chipmunks, and squirrels, especially Fox and

Gray (tree) squirrels and flying squirrels, can be effective predators, especially on bird eggs and nestlings.

But of all the predators that our American Robin is likely to encounter, none is as effective as the domestic house cat. Tyler reports that "a cat will capture, on the average, 50 birds in a season, and the helpless young robins provide a large part of the kill." Domestic house cats, escaped or allowed to run free, have become so common in the suburbs that they take thousands of robins and other songbirds yearly.

Tyler's estimate may be extremely low, according to a 1974 article in *The Wilson Bulletin* by William George. He reports that birds are a significant part of the house cat's prey base: 20 percent in California, 18 percent in Pennsylvania, 12 percent in Maryland and Missouri, 11 percent in Texas and Wisconsin, and 3 percent in Michigan. These figures average more than 10 percent per state. In another study, University of Wisconsin ornithologist Stanley Temple estimated that 20 million to 150 million songbirds are killed each and every year by rural house cats in Wisconsin alone. Paul Fluck, in a 1949 article published in *Louisiana Conservationist,* claims that domestic house cats kill more birds, especially ground nesters and newly fledged songbirds, than any of our native predators. Fluck also blames house cats for the nationwide decline in quail and several other huntable species.

The 1991 edition of *The Encyclopedia Americana International* states that 58 million house cats are kept as pets in the United States. A little arithmetic can readily provide some startling figures. If even half of 58 million cats (29 million) are allowed outdoors for any amount of time at all, they will kill 29 million birds annually, and many house cats kill multiple birds every day. A good many of those will undoubtedly be American Robins.

Further, a 1989 "Dear Abby" column referred to a chart from the Maryland Society for the Prevention of Cruelty to Animals on the reproductive potential of uncontrolled domestic house cat populations: "Two uncontrolled breeding cats— plus all their kittens and all their kittens' kittens, if none are ever neutered or spayed, add up to: first year: 12; second year: 66; third year: 382; fourth year: 2,201; fifth year: 12,680; sixth year: 73,041; seventh year: 420,715; eighth year: 2,423,316; ninth year: 13,958,290. Boggles your mind, doesn't it?"

In summary, George H. Lowery, Jr., in *The Mammals of Louisiana and Its Adjacent Waters,* states, "One of the greatest decimators of wildlife, particularly of song birds, are feral cats or 'tabbies' that are allowed outside the house. People who take unwanted cats to the outskirts of town and release them to feed for themselves are doing irresponsible harm to the bird populations in these areas."

Competitors

Competitors are not so deadly to robins as the domestic house cat and hawk, but they nevertheless can seriously undermine the robin's ability to feed its family adequately. Gulls and jaegers are best known for their habit of forcing smaller birds to drop their food, but C. M. Arnold observed a House Sparrow following a robin about and snatching earthworms away before it could carry them off to waiting youngsters (Bent). Bent also provides us with a quotation from L. P. Bolander, Jr., about competing gulls:

> I observed a Glaucous-winged Gull, three California Gulls and one Ring-billed Gull standing on the grass plot amid about eighty robins. Every time a robin would start pulling out a worm a gull would make a run toward him. Of course the robin would let go of the worm and then the gull would gobble it up! This was repeated again and again. . . . Sometimes the worm would come out quickly enough for the robin to get it down before the gull could get on the job. If the worm was too big for the robin to swallow immediately the gull would pursue it, and the robin usually dived under a protecting oak tree or madrone. The gull would not follow there.

Nest competitors are few and far between, but they do appear occasionally. For instance, both Mourning Doves and House

Sparrows are known to evict robins from their nests. They then construct their own nests on top.

Brood Parasites

American Robins are seldom affected by brood parasites, namely the Brown-headed Cowbird, a bird that isn't capable of rearing its own young so it lays eggs in other birds' nests. Our robin is generally considered a rejecter species, one that is able to recognize the eggs of other birds and discard them. In Illinois, Richard and Jean Graber and Ethelyn Kirk found, in a sample of 400 robin nests, only one cowbird egg in a nest with three host eggs. They report that "the host was successful in fledging young, but the cowbird egg disappeared."

The reasons robins are seldom victims of nest parasitism vary, but undoubtedly an important factor is their keen ability to recognize foreign eggs that possess a different size, color, pattern, or shape. Plus, the size of a robin nestling also tends to provide plenty of nest competition for a baby cowbird. Although a baby cowbird can shove its way around and outcompete smaller warblers, vireos, and many other songbirds, our American Robin baby will simply overpower, even smother, a smaller cowbird baby.

The Bronzed Cowbird, however, a larger bird that effectively parasitizes orioles, undoubtedly also preys on American Robins. Because the robin's North American breeding range only casually overlaps that of the more tropical Bronzed Cowbird, it is not currently considered a significant factor, but as the adaptable robin continues to expand its breeding range southward, the Bronzed Cowbird probably will become a factor.

Overindulgence

There are very few records of robins dying from eating natural, nontoxic foods. There are, however, a few cases of birds that have indulged on fermented fruit and then, inebriated, flown into the path of a passing vehicle or against a windowpane. An excessive amount of several fermented fruits can pose a serious threat. For instance, large doses of the juice of ornamental Tatarian honeysuckle berries can cause cardiac paralysis in birds, and the fermented fruits of Chinaberry can attack the bird's central nervous system.

Weather

Storms are also a constant threat, but one that birds normally cope with reasonably well. A July tornado at Portsmouth, Iowa, however, killed 71 robins, and a severe electrical storm killed about 50 robins that were roosting in a tree hit by lightning. Some nests are dislodged by violent windstorms. Hail, too, can have devastating effects on the American Robin, which spends so much time in the open.

One cannot help but wonder about migrating robin flocks that chance upon a late season storm. I am reminded of a pertinent Aldo Leopold description, from *A Sand County Almanac,* about migrating geese: "One swallow does not make a summer, but one skein of geese, cleaving the murk of a March thaw, is the spring. . . . A chipmunk, emerging for a sunbath but finding a blizzard, has only to go back to bed. But a migrating goose, stalking two hundred miles of black night on the chance of finding a hole in the lake, has no easy chance of retreat. His arrival carries the conviction of a prophet who has burned his bridges."

Diseases

Robin deaths from disease are extremely difficult to detect, but a few have been recorded. Bacterial diseases, such as avian cholera, botulism, tuberculosis, salmonellosis, and chlamydiosis; viral diseases, such as avian pox; fungal diseases, such as aspergillosis; parasitic diseases, such as sarcocystis and gizzard worms; and toxic diseases, such as oil toxicosis, do occur in songbirds, although they are rare or infrequent. The highest-probability diseases are tuberculosis, salmonellosis, pox, and aspergillosis. Birds with avian tuberculosis appear weak and lethargic, often with diarrhea and lameness, and they may develop abscesses and nodular growths around the eyes, legs, side of face, and base of beak, according to Thomas J. Roffe. Avian salmonellosis causes drowsiness and diarrhea, and birds "tremble and gasp for air, their wings often droop and they sometimes stagger and fall over before death. These birds often have pasted vents and eyelids that are swollen and stuck together by a fluid discharge" (Stroud and Friend 1987). Birds with avian pox usually possess wartlike nodules on the "featherless areas of their bodies, including feet, legs, base of the beak, and eye margin" (Hansen 1987). "The typical aspergillosis-affected bird is emaciated and frequently manifests severe and progressive difficulty in breathing by gaping (rapid opening and closing of the bill). Birds often appear to be unthrifty, and wing-droop may occur" (Locke 1987).

Human-caused Deaths

Human-caused deaths are not only senseless but also illegal. Shooting and trapping of robins and numerous other birds were once commonplace in North America. Until all migratory birds received legal protection through the Migratory Bird Conservation Act of 1929, millions of songbirds were killed annually for food. Huge flocks of wintering robins were shot for the marketplace during the 1800s. One is reminded of the line of an old English nursery rhyme, "Four and twenty blackbirds baked in a pie," which actually referred to the European Blackbird, a closely related European thrush. John James Audubon, who apparently favored the practice of shooting songbirds for food, reported in 1841:

> In all the southern states, . . . their presence [American Robins] is productive of a sort of jubilee among the gunners, and the

havoc made among them with bows and arrows, blowguns, and traps of different sorts, is wonderful. Every gunner brings them home by bagsful, and the markets are supplied with them at a very cheap rate. Several persons may at this season stand round the foot of a tree loaded with berries, and shoot the greater part of the day, so fast do the flocks of Robins succeed each other. They are then fat and juicy, and afford excellent eating. (Bent 1964)

Some shooting of songbirds still occurs for the purpose of protecting crops. In 1973, eight cranberry growers shot an estimated 20,000 American robins that were feeding on their fields; "one man shot 7,000 on his 200-acre farm alone," according to Bent. Robins can do considerable damage to cherry, grape, olive, and tomato crops, especially on their wintering grounds. Biologists have studied methods of scaring the birds away but have not found an effective and economical solution. Acoustic bird-scare devices, shooting, and netting are all effective, but they cost far more than the damaged crops.

Of all the human causes of mortality, none has caused so much consternation as the artificial biocides invented to control pests. Although there undoubtedly is some good that results from the use of some poisons, such as the near elimination of malaria in many parts of the world and the control of boll weevils in our cotton fields, the effects on secondary consumers are often disastrous.

The best known of the deadly biocides is DDT, a long-lived chemical that penetrates the integument of any insect that it contacts. This and other persistent poisons "have led to the phenomenon of biological magnification, whereby the concentration of the toxic substance increases progressively to the highest trophic levels," according to Lorus and Margery Milne, in *The Arena of Life: The Dynamics of Ecology*. They also correctly point out that "fully half of the pesticide misses the target animals. It blows away as dust, or washes into the nearest stream. It destroys natural predators and parasites, which would otherwise help control the pest, and kills harmless and beneficial organisms alike, upsetting many food webs unrelated to the pests."

DDT totally wiped out the Eastern Peregrine Falcon and seriously threatened other peregrines, the Brown Pelican, Bald Eagle, Osprey, and a host of other creatures at the top of the food chain. It was not until the American public became aware of the possible extinction of the American Robin, because DDT causes paralysis of its central nervous system, that something was finally done to save it and other sensitive species. DDT eventually was banned for use in the United States and Canada in 1972.

It was the American Robin that became the symbol of the fight to stop the use of this deadly chemical. Rachael Carson's book *Silent Spring* was the springboard for action. Carson wrote eloquently about the effects of DDT on our wild creatures. She begins her book thus: "It was a spring without voices. On the mornings that had once throbbed with the dawn chorus of robins, catbirds, doves, jays, wrens, and scores of other birds' voices, there was now no sound; only silence lay over the fields and woods and marsh." She also writes how the spraying of DDT, used to kill Dutch elm disease at Michigan State University, decimated robin populations there: "Several facts suggested that the robins were being poisoned, not so much by direct contact with the insecticides as indirectly, by eating earthworms. Campus earthworms had been fed to crayfish in a research project and all the crayfish had promptly died. A snake in a laboratory cage had gone into violent tremors after being fed such worms. And earthworms are the principal food of robins in the spring."

Carson goes on to explain that further studies traced "the intricate cycle of events by which robins are linked to the elm trees by way of the earthworms." The trees were sprayed each spring with DDT to kill various target species, such as bark beetles and other insects and spiders. The poison forms a film on the leaves and bark that remains throughout the summer. But when the leaves fall to the ground in the autumn, they accumulate in layers and begin to decay. The leaf litter is a favorite food of earthworms, which help to break them down into soil. In swallowing the leaves, they also swallow the insecticide that accumulates in their bodies. While some of the earthworms die, others survive to become biological magnifiers of the poison.

Robins return in the spring to nest and feed on earthworms. Research showed that as "few as 11 large earthworms can transfer a lethal dose of DDT to a robin. And 11 worms form a small part of a day's rations to a bird that eats 10 to 12 earthworms in as many minutes," according to Carson. Although every robin nest under observation in 1954 produced young (370), only one young robin could be found in the same area in 1957. The studies by Carson and her colleagues at Michigan State, and duplicated at other locations, provided the evidence necessary to convince the public of the deadly consequences of DDT.

The 1972 ban of DDT use in the United States and Canada began a new era of environmental awareness, and within a dozen years many of the affected species began to recover. Today, the Brown Pelican and American Robin have fully recovered, and populations of Bald Eagle, Osprey, and Peregrine Falcon are well on their way.

Robin nest on a built platform.
Photo by Maslowski Wildlife Productions.

Inviting Robins
to Your Home

ALTHOUGH there is little that can be done to encourage American Robins to remain and nest outside their normal breeding grounds, there are several things that can be done to support those that do nest nearby. Construction of a robin shelf, placed under the protective eaves of the house, barn, or shed, can have positive results. The shelf should have a floor of at least 6 by 8 inches and a sloping roof. Walter Schutz, in *How to Attract, House, and Feed Birds,* recommends an open shelf of 8.5 by 7.5 inches, with a back of 8.5 by 9.5 inches and a roof of 7.5 by 10.5 inches.

Nesting robins also may take advantage of various nesting materials that can easily be supplied. For instance, pieces of string or yarn placed in the open or in a suspended wire basket may readily be utilized. However, cut the pieces into strips not more than 12 inches in length, or the birds may end up getting tangled in their own nesting materials. Also, if the weather is dry so that mud is not readily available, you can either mix up a bowl of mud or make a special muddy place in your yard.

Plantings also can be effective for attracting robins year-round. Michael McKinley, in *How to Attract Birds,* lists favorite landscape plants for the American Robin: trees include crab apple, hackberry, hawthorn, hemlock, maple, mulberry, persimmon, sassafras, and tupelo; large shrubs and small trees include buckthorn, juniper, cherry, dogwood, elaeagnus, holly, serviceberry, and sumac; low shrubs and vines include barberry, bittersweet, blackberry, raspberry, blueberry, elderberry, firethorn (pyracantha), grape, honeysuckle, rose, spicebush, viburnum, and Virginia creeper.

Feeding stations can be stocked for robins at various times of the year. Fresh fruit, such as almost any berry, apples, bananas, raisins, and even olives, will be consumed. They also will eat bread and cooked spaghetti, and even a bone with scraps of meat on it is welcome. Heppner kept caged robins during his research on the bird's clues to locating earthworms, maintaining them on an artificial diet:

> A diet which was acceptable to all birds consisted of a gruel composed of one-half minced apple thickened with Gerber's high protein baby food, one-eighth cup of raisins, and two drops of Stewart's vitamin formula. The birds preferred minced apples to sliced apples. Each bird was given five to ten earthworms per day. Two birds were maintained for eleven months on this diet, and were released in good condition at the end of the experiments.

Whatever the available foods may be, the best attractant of our American Robin is water. Whether the water is in a birdbath or pond, robins will drink and bathe whenever it is available. Birdbaths must be shallow, an inch or less in depth, to attract songbirds. The smallest yard usually can afford space for a birdbath. If space is not a limiting factor, ponds and larger pools can increase the potential for attracting robins and other wildlife.

Moving or dripping water attracts more birds than a quiet birdbath. I have run a small rubber tube underground from a nearby faucet to a tree overshadowing my birdbath. By running the tube up the tree trunk, fairly well hidden in the grooves of my live oak, I positioned the tube so that it drips about four feet into the water of a raised birdbath. The splashing sounds actually attract migrants that would not otherwise become aware of the water. I have also placed a secondary, ground-level birdbath below the raised one so that water will drip into that one as well. This gives birds two options; I have found that robins will use the ground-level birdbath first and take advantage of the raised birdbath only when the lower one is mobbed with other bathing robins.

In Closing

THE American Robin is unquestionably North America's most widespread songbird, present in the far north during the summer months, throughout most of the United States year-round, and common in the southern parts of its range at least in winter. The result of this continentwide distribution is that the American Robin is our most familiar bird; it is the official state bird for Connecticut, Michigan, and Wisconsin; it is featured on Canada's two-dollar bills; and every child learns to recognize it almost before walking.

The robin's familiar features—its robin-red breast, upright posture, and loud, ringing songs—are significant parts of our earliest outdoor memories. No other bird sings so many hours of the day and for so long a period of time. Its size, breast color, robin's-egg blue eggs, and flutelike caroling are standard-setters in the bird world.

Robins also may be our most adaptable songbird, seeking out new breeding grounds whenever possible and adjusting to an amazing diversity of food, from a wide variety of small animals to fruits of many kinds. Robins use our lawns and gardens during the nesting season, our berry trees, shrubs, and vines in summer, fall, and winter, and our birdbaths whenever possible. They are one of our most courageous songbirds, defending their nests and nestlings against a host of threats.

All of these highlights conclusively prove that the American Robin is truly our most visible and beloved songbird.

Bibliography

Allen, Glover M. 1925. *Birds and Their Attributes*. Boston: Marshall Jones Co.

American Ornithologists' Union. 1983. *Check-list of North American Birds*. 6th ed. Washington, D.C.: American Ornithologists' Union.

Austin, Oliver L., Jr. 1967. *Song Birds of the World*. New York: Golden Press.

Bailey, Alfred M., and Robert J. Niedrack. 1936. Community Nesting of Western Robins and House Finches. *Condor* 38:214–215.

Ball, Alice E. 1937. *American Land Birds*. New York: Tudor Publishing.

Barrows, Walter Bradford. 1912. *Michigan Bird Life*. Lansing: Michigan Agricultural College.

Bean, Michael J. 1983. *The Evolution of National Wildlife Law*. New York: Praeger.

Bent, Arthur Cleveland, ed. 1964. *Life Histories of North American Thrushes, Kinglets, and Their Allies*. New York: Dover.

Brandt, Herbert. 1951. *Arizona and Its Bird Life*. Cleveland: Bird Research Foundation.

Bruun, Bertel. 1978. *The Larousse Guide to Birds of Britain and Europe*. New York: Larousse.

Burroughs, John. 1893. *Wake-Robin*. Boston: Houghton Mifflin.

———. 1913. *The Summit of the Years*. Boston: Houghton Mifflin.

Carson, Rachel. 1962. *Silent Spring*. Greenwich, Conn.: Fawcett.

Charles, Fred L. 1909. Some Observations on Robin Nests. *Illinois Academy of Science Transactions* 2:27–31.

Collias, Nicholas E., and Elsie C. Collias. 1984. *Nest Building and Bird Behavior*. Princeton, N.J.: Princeton University Press.

Collins, Henry H., Jr., and Ned R. Boyajians. 1965. *Familiar Garden Birds of America*. New York: Harper & Row.

Corral, Michael. 1989. *The World of Birds: A Layman's Guide to Ornithology*. Chester, Conn.: Globe Pequot Press.

Davidson, Verne E. 1967. *Attracting Birds from the Prairies to the Atlantic*. New York: Thomas Y. Crowell Co.

A Dictionary of American Proverbs, eds. Wolfgang Mieder, Stewart A. Kingbury, and Kelsie B. Harden. 1992. New York: Oxford University Press.

Doolittle, Thomas C. J. 1992. Status of the Eastern Taiga Merlin *Falco c. columbianus.* Master's thesis, University of Wisconsin, Eau Claire.

Dorst, Jean. 1974. *The Life of Birds.* Vol. 1. New York: Columbia University Press.

Dunson, William A. 1965. Adaptation of Heart and Lung Weight to High Altitude in the Robin. *Condor* 67:215–219.

Ehrlich, Paul R., David S. Dobkin, and Darryl Wheye. 1988. *The Birder's Handbook.* New York: Simon & Schuster.

Eiserer, L. A. 1976. *The American Robin: A Backyard Institution.* Chicago: Nelson Hall.

Farley, Frank L. 1932. *Birds of the Battle River Region.* Edmondton: Institute of Applied Art.

Farner, Donald S. 1945. Age Groups and Longevity in the American Robin. *Wilson Bulletin* 57 (1): 56–74.

Finlay, J. Cam. 1994. Hearing Aids for Birders. *Bird Watcher's Digest* Nov.–Dec.: 48–51.

Fluck, Paul H. 1949. Prince of Pests. *Louisiana Conservationist* Sept.: 6–7, 26.

Flyger, Vagn, and J. Edward Gates. 1982. Fox and Gray Squirrels. In *Wild Mammals of North America,* ed. Joseph A. Chapman and George A. Feldhamer. Baltimore: Johns Hopkins University Press.

Forbush, Edward Howe. 1929. *Birds of Massachusetts and Other New England States.* Norwood, Mass: Norwood Press.

Gabrielson, Ira N., and Stanley G. Jewett. 1940. *Birds of Oregon.* Corvallis: Oregon State College.

Gabrielson, Ira N., and Frederick C. Lincoln. 1959. *Birds of Alaska.* Harrisburg, Penn.: Stackpole.

George, William G. 1974. Domestic Cats as Predators and Factors in Winter Shortage of Raptor Prey. *Wilson Bulletin* 86 (4): 384–396.

Gifford, Jerome. 1984. 155: Campground in Old Orchards. *American Birds* 38 (1): 114.

Godfrey, W. Earl. 1966. *The Birds of Canada.* Ottawa: National Museums of Canada.

Graber, Richard R., Jean W. Graber, and Ethelyn L. Kirk. 1971. *Illinois Birds: Turdidae.* Urbana: Illinois Natural History Survey.

Graham, Frank, Jr. 1970. *Since Silent Spring.* Boston: Houghton Mifflin.

————. 1994. What Is the State of State Birds? *American Birds* Spring: 64–69.

————. 1995. Unnatural Predation. *Audubon* Nov.–Dec.: 84–89.

Gruson, Edward S. 1972. *Words for Birds: A Lexicon of North American Birds with Biogeographical Notes.* New York: Quadrangle Books.

Hansen, Wallace R. 1987. Avian Pox. In *Field Guide to Wildlife Diseases,* ed. Milton Friend. USDI, Fish and Wildlife Series Resource Publication 167, GPO.

Headstrom, Richard. 1970. *A Complete Field Guide to Nests in the United States.* New York: Ives Washburn.

Henshaw, H. W. 1875. Report upon the Ornithological Collections Made in Portions of Nevada, Utah, California, Colorado, New Mexico, and Arizona during the Years 1871, 1872, 1873, and 1874. In *Report upon Geographical and Geological Explorations and Surveys West of the One Hundredth Meridian.* Washington, D.C.: GPO.

Heppner, Frank. 1965. Sensory Mechanisms and Environmental Clues Used by the American Robin in Locating Earthworms. *Condor* 67 (3): 247–256.

Howell, Joseph C. 1942. Habits of the American Robin. *American Midland Naturalists* 28 (3): 529–603.

Hudson, Robert A. 1984. 156: Scattered Mixed Coniferous Forest in Subalpine Meadows and Spruce Bogs. *American Birds* 38 (1): 114–115.

Imhof, Thomas A. 1984. 94: Suburban Cemetery. *American Birds* 38 (1): 95–96.

Jones, J. Knox, David M. Armstrong, and Jerry R. Choate. 1985. *Guide to Mammals of the Plains States.* Lincoln: University of Nebraska Press.

Karpus, Martin. 1952. Bird Activity in the Continuous Daylight of Arctic Summer. *Ecology* 33 (1): 129–134.

Lane, Frank W. 1957. *Animal Wonder World.* Greenwich, Conn.: Fawcett.

————. 1961. *Nature Parade: The Private Lives of Animals.* Greenwich, Conn.: Fawcett.

Lasley, Greg W., and Mike Krzywonski. 1991. First United States Record of the White-throated Robin. *American Birds* Summer: 230–231.

Lawrence, R. D. 1974. *Wildlife in North America: Birds.* Radnor, Penn.: Chilton Book.

Leopold, Aldo. 1966. *A Sand County Almanac.* New York: Oxford University Press.

Leopold, Aldo, and Alfred E. Eynon. 1961. Avian Daylight and Evening Song in Relation to Time and Light Intensity. *Condor* 63:269–293.

Locke, Louis N. 1987. Aspergillosis. In *Field Guide to Wildlife Diseases*, ed. Milton Friend. USDI, Fish and Wildlife Series Resource Publication 167, GPO.

Long, R. Charles. 1989. American Robin. In *Hinterland Who's Who*. Canada Wildlife Service, Environment Canada.

Lowery, George H., Jr. 1974a. *Louisiana Birds*. Baton Rouge: Louisiana State University Press.

———. 1974b. *The Mammals of Louisiana and Its Adjacent Waters*. Baton Rouge: Louisiana State University Press.

Lowther, Peter E. 1981. American Robin Rears Brown-headed Cowbird. *Journal of Field Ornithology* 52 (2): 45–47.

Martin, Alexander C., Herbert S. Zim, and Arnold L. Nelson. 1951. *American Wildlife and Plants: A Guide to Wildlife Food Habits*. New York: Dover.

Martin, Laura C. 1993. *The Folklore of Birds*. Old Saybrook, Conn.: Globe Pequot Press.

McKinley, Michael. 1983. *How to Attract Birds*. San Francisco: Ortho Books.

Merriam, Florence A. 1898. *Birds of Village and Field*. Boston: Houghton Mifflin.

Milne, Lorus, and Margery Milne. 1971. *The Arena of Life: The Dynamics of Ecology*. Garden City, N.Y.: Doubleday.

Morse, Charles M. 1931. Kingbirds and Robins. *Bird Lore* 33:260.

Murray, J. J. 1930. A Robin's Nesting. *Bird Lore* 35:428.

Norris, R. A., and F. S. Williamson. 1955. Variation in Relative Heart Size of Certain Passerines with Increase in Altitude. *Wilson Bulletin* 67:78–83.

Oberholser, Harry C. 1974. *The Bird Life of Texas*. Vol. 2. Austin: University of Texas Press.

Opie, Iona, and Peter Opie. 1973. *The Oxford Dictionary of Nursery Rhymes*. Oxford: Oxford University Press.

Opie, Iona, and Moira Tatem. 1989. *A Dictionary of Superstitions*. Oxford: Oxford University Press.

Pasquier, Roger F. 1980. *Watching Birds: An Introduction to Ornithology*. Boston: Houghton Mifflin.

Paszkowski, Cynthia A. 1982. Vegetation, Ground, and Frugivorous Foraging of the American Robin. *Auk* 99:701–709.

Peterson, P. C. 1965. (Winter Season) Middlewestern Prairie Region. *Audubon Field Notes* 10 (3): 232–233.

Raney, Edward C. 1939. Robin and Mourning Dove Use the Same Nest. *Auk* 56:337–338.

Robbins, Chandler S. 1956. Changing Seasons: A Summary of the Winter Season. *Audubon Field Notes* 10 (3): 232–233.

Robbins, Chandler S., Danny Bystrak, and Paul H. Geissler. 1986. *The Breeding Bird Survey: Its First Fifteen Years, 1965–1979*. Washington, D.C.: U.S. Fish and Wildlife Service.

Roffe, Thomas J. 1987. Avian Tuberculosis. In *Field Guide to Wildlife Diseases*, ed. Milton Friend. USDI, Fish and Wildlife Series Resource Publication 167, GPO.

Root, Terry. 1988. *Atlas of Wintering North American Birds: An Analysis of Christmas Bird Count Data*. Chicago: University of Chicago Press.

Ryser, Fred A., Jr. 1985. *Birds of the Great Basin: A Natural History*. Reno: University of Nevada Press.

Saunders, Aretas A. 1964. *An Introduction to Bird Life for Bird Watchers*. New York: Dover.

Schantz, William Edward. 1939. A Detailed Study of a Family of Robins. *Wilson Bulletin* 51 (3): 157–169.

Schutz, Walter E. 1970. *How to Attract, House, and Feed Birds*. New York: Bruce Publishing.

Shakespeare, William. 1936. *The Complete Works of William Shakespeare*. Cambridge Edition, ed. William Aldis Wright. Garden City, N.Y.: Garden City Books.

Sharp, Millard H. 1990. America's Songbird. *Wild Bird* May: 22–29.

Sprunt, Alexander, Jr. 1955. *North American Birds of Prey*. New York: Harper & Bros.

Stokes, Donald W. 1979. *A Guide to the Behavior of Common Birds*. Boston: Little, Brown.

Stone, Witmer. 1965. *Bird Studies at Old Cape May*. Vol. 2. New York: Dover.

Storer, Tracy Irwin. 1926. Range Extensions by the Western Robin in California. *Condor* 28:264–267.

Stroud, Richard K., and Milton Friend. 1987. Avian Salmonella. In *Field Guide to Wildlife Diseases*, ed. Milton Friend. USDI, Fish and Wildlife Series Resource Publication 167, GPO.

Stupka, Arthur. 1963. *Notes on the Birds of Great Smoky Mountains National Park*. Knoxville: University of Tennessee Press.

Sumner, Lowell, and Joseph S. Dixon. 1953. *Birds and Mammals of the Sierra Nevada*. Berkeley: University of California Press.

Sutton, George Miksch. 1986. *Birds Worth Watching*. Norman: University of Oklahoma Press.

Taft, John E. 1970. Possible Seven-Day Incubation Period in the Robin, *Turdus migratorius*. *Audubon Field Notes* 24 (5): 652.

Tazik, David J. 1984. 183: Abandoned Farmland. *American Birds* 38 (1): 123.

Temple, Stanley A. 1977. *Endangered Birds: Management Techniques for Preserving Threatened Species*. Madison: University of Wisconsin Press.

Terres, John K. 1987. *The Audubon Society Encyclopedia of North American Birds*. New York: Alfred A. Knopf.

Tinbergen, Niko. 1958. *Curious Naturalist*. New York: Basic Books.

Toups, Judith A., and Jerome A. Jackson. 1987. *Birds and Birding on the Mississippi Coast*. Jackson: University Press of Mississippi.

Trenary, Don C. 1945. That Cheerful Songster, the Robin. *Science Digest* 35 (4): 7–10.

Tyler, Winsor Marrett. 1964. Eastern Robin. In *Life Histories of North American Thrushes, Kinglets, and Their Allies*, ed. Arthur Cleveland Bent. New York: Dover.

Van Horn, Don. 1984. 134: Douglas-Fir–Ponderosa Pine Forest. *American Birds* 38 (1): 107.

Vanwoerkom, Gordon J. 1996. Robin Hoodlum. *Birder's World* June: 88.

Walsberg, Glenn E., and James R. King. 1980. The Thermoregulatory Significance of the Winter Roost Sites Selected by Robins in Eastern Washington. *Wilson Bulletin* 92 (1): 33–39.

Wauer, Roland H. 1962. Birds of Death Valley National Monument. Unpublished manuscript.

———. 1991. Profiles of an ABA Birder. *Birding* June: 146–154.

———. 1992. *The Visitor's Guide to the Birds of the Eastern National Parks: United States and Canada*. Santa Fe, N.Mex.: John Muir Publications.

———. 1993. *The Visitor's Guide to the Birds of the Rocky Mountain National Parks: United States and Canada*. Santa Fe, N.Mex.: John Muir Publications.

———. 1994. *The Visitor's Guide to the Birds of the Central National Parks: United States and Canada*. Santa Fe, N.Mex.: John Muir Publications.

Webster, John. 1966. The White Devil. In *The Revel Plays*, ed. John Russell Brown. London: Methuen.

Welty, Joel Carl. 1975. *The Life of Birds.* Philadelphia: W. B. Saunders Co.

Wetherbee, Kenneth B. 1930. Cooperative Parents. *Bird Lore* 32:202.

Wharton, William. 1979. *Birdy.* New York: Alfred A. Knopf.

Wheelwright, Nathaniel T. 1986. The Distribution of American Robins: An Analysis of U.S. Biological Survey Records. *Auk* 103:710–725.

Wolffsohn, Marguerite, and William J. Kolodnicki. 1984. 189: Suburban Bird Sanctuary. *American Birds* 38 (1): 125–126.

Yoder-Williams, Michael P., and Kimberly With. 1984. 139: Mixed Conifer Forest. *American Birds* 38 (1): 109.

Young, H. 1955. Breeding Behavior and Nesting of the Eastern Robin. *American Midland Naturalist* 53:329–352.